PENGUIN BOOKS

Imagist Poetry

Peter Jones was born in Walsall, West Midlands, in 1929 and educated at the local grammar school and at Oxford University. He taught English and Classics at Christ's Hospital until 1969. In 1970 he co-founded Carcanet Press and became its Managing Director. His published books of poetry include *Rain*, *Seagarden for Julius*, *The Peace and The Hook*, and *The Garden End*. His critical works include an introduction to H.D.'s *Tribute to Freud*, *An Introduction to Fifty American Poets*, *Shakespeare: The Sonnets – A Casebook*, and he is co-editor of *British Poetry Since 1970: A Critical Survey*.

READ MORE IN PENGUIN

A SELECTION OF POETRY

American Verse
British Poetry since 1945
Caribbean Verse in English
Chinese Love Poetry
A Choice of Comic and Curious Verse
Contemporary American Poetry
Contemporary British Poetry
Contemporary Irish Poetry
Earliest English Poems
English Romantic Verse
English Verse
First World War Poetry
French Poetry
German Verse
Greek Verse
Hebrew Verse
Imagist Poetry
Irish Verse
Japanese Verse
Medieval English Lyrics
The Metaphysical Poets
Modern African Poetry
New Poetry
Nineteenth Century American Poetry
Poetry of the Thirties
Restoration Verse
Scottish Verse
Surrealist Poetry in English
Spanish Verse
Victorian Verse
Women Poets
Zen Poetry

IMAGIST POETRY

Introduced and edited
by
Peter Jones

PENGUIN BOOKS

PENGUIN BOOKS

Published by the Penguin Group

Penguin Books Ltd, 80 Strand, London WC2R ORL, England
Penguin Group (USA) Inc., 375 Hudson Street, New York, New York 10014, USA
Penguin Group (Canada), 90 Eglinton Avenue East, Suite 700, Toronto, Ontario, Canada M4P 2Y3
(a division of Pearson Penguin Canada Inc.)
Penguin Ireland, 25 St Stephen's Green, Dublin 2, Ireland (a division of Penguin Books Ltd)
Penguin Group (Australia), 250 Camberwell Road, Camberwell, Victoria 3124, Australia
(a division of Pearson Australia Group Pty Ltd)
Penguin Books India Pvt Ltd, 11 Community Centre, Panchsheel Park, New Delhi – 110 017, India
Penguin Group (NZ), 67 Apollo Drive, Rosedale, North Shore 0632, New Zealand
(a division of Pearson New Zealand Ltd)
Penguin Books (South Africa) (Pty) Ltd, 24 Sturdee Avenue, Rosebank, Johannesburg 2196, South Africa

Penguin Books Ltd, Registered Offices: 80 Strand, London WC2R ORL, England

www.penguin.com

First published in Penguin Books 1972
Reprinted in Penguin Classics 2001

019

Copyright © Peter Jones, 1972
All rights reserved

Printed in England by Clays Ltd, St Ives plc
Set in Monotype Bembo

www.greenpenguin.co.uk

MIX
Paper from
responsible sources
FSC
www.fsc.org **FSC® C018179**

Penguin Books is committed to a sustainable
future for our business, our readers and our planet.
This book is made from Forest Stewardship
Council™ certified paper.

for Michael Schmidt

CONTENTS

THE IMAGISTS AFTER IMAGISM

INTRODUCTION

Sir: May I beg for a clear definition of the word 'Imagisme', as well as information as to whether it be in French, American or Colonial language? If it were in English, would there be the 'e' at the end? I do not think that Ezra Pound can be an American, as he does not shun the 'subjunctive mood' – Yours truly, A. E. F. Horniman.

(We believe that 'Imagisme' comes from a city which all good Americans are supposed to visit late or soon ... ED)

Letter in T.P.'s Weekly, 6 March 1915.

To cope with the Imagists should be an easy matter. We have their four annual anthologies 1914–17; we have a detailed manifesto in 1915 stating their intentions; and there is a fifth anthology in 1930 to let us know how they were faring as individuals thirteen years after the break-up of the group. There were only seven poets intimately associated with the movement – four Americans (Ezra Pound, Hilda Doolittle, John Gould Fletcher, Amy Lowell) and three British (Richard Aldington, F. S. Flint, D. H. Lawrence). Perhaps one ought simply to look at the manifesto and the anthologies and forget such introductions as this.

But the movement is riddled with paradox. To begin with, the poems in the anthologies often don't tally with the precepts of the manifesto (which are we to believe – practice or theory?). One of the poets, D. H. Lawrence, appeared both in the imagist anthologies and in those of a group whose theory and practice were totally different – the Georgians[1] (could he honestly follow both?). The founder-poet, Ezra Pound, left the movement after its first year. And innumerable seemingly conflicting definitions of 'the image' have proliferated over the years. Perhaps the main problem is that the poems the Imagists published as a group cannot honestly be called to stand among the great achievements of literature. Some are very fine, but many are weak by any standards. And so why bother?

Part of the answer lies in a statement made by T. S. Eliot in an

address on 'American Literature and the American Language' in
1953: 'The *point de repère* usually and conveniently taken as the
starting-point of modern poetry is the group denominated "imagists"
in London about 1910.'[2] Their historical importance is clear. And a
notice of their 1916 anthology in *The Times Literary Supplement* gives
us the other part of the answer: 'Imagist poetry fills us with hope;
even when it is not very good in itself, it seems to promise a form in
which very good poetry could be written.'[3] The truth is that imagistic
ideas still lie at the centre of our poetic practice.

The parlous state of poetry at the turn of the century is evident from
the number of groups dedicated to rebellion and reform – the
Georgians, the Futurists, the Imagists and the Vorticists among the
most prominent. Ford Madox Hueffer (later changing his name to
Ford Madox Ford) wrote in 1913: '... the song of birds, moonlight –
these the poet playing for safety and the critic trying to find something
to praise, will deem the sure cards of the poetic pack. They seem the
safe things to sentimentalise over and it is taken for granted that
sentimentality is the business of poetry.'[4] Ezra Pound was charac-
teristically much more forceful in his condemnation: 'The common
verse in Britain from 1890 was a horrible agglomerate compost, not
minted, most of it not even baked, all legato, a doughy mess of third-
hand Keats, Wordsworth, heaven knows what, fourth-hand Eliza-
bethan sonority blunted, half-melted, lumpy.'[5] Pound had already
published in 1909 a poem called 'Revolt Against the Crepuscular
Spirit in Modern Poetry':

> Great God, if men are grown but pale sick phantoms
>   That must live only in these mists and tempered lights
> ... if these thy sons are grown such thin ephemera.
> I bid thee grapple chaos ...[6]

It needed perhaps an outsider to see a way through all this. Such a
man was T. E. Hulme – a mathematics student sent down from
Cambridge in 1904 for unspecified riotous behaviour. Abandoning a
course in biology at London University in the same year, he travelled
by cargo boat to Canada and there, as he worked his way across the
country, he was overwhelmed by the sight of the vast prairie land:

'. . . the first time', he wrote, 'I ever felt the necessity or inevitableness of verse, was in the desire to produce the peculiar quality of feeling which is induced by the flat spaces and wide horizons of the virgin-prairie of Western Canada.'[7] He returned to Europe determined to learn more of the art of literature; and turning to philosophy as well, in 1907 he began studies of Henri Bergson, Rémy de Gourmont and Jules de Gaultier, in Brussels. By 1908 he had begun to form his own theories of poetry, and gathered around himself a group drawn from the literary society of London to discuss literary matters. They called themselves the Poets' Club. T. E. Hulme had written a few poems to illustrate his theories, and no doubt they were read out and discussed at the meetings of the Club. None of the later Imagists was a member of this group, but the poems 'Autumn' and 'A City Sunset' by Hulme, which the Poets' Club printed in January 1909 in a booklet called *For Christmas MDCCCCVIII*, may reasonably be termed the first 'imagist' poems, although the word itself was not yet in use.

Both the Poets' Club and its publication received a sharp notice from F. S. Flint in a periodical called *The New Age*. He objected to the Club's 'after dinner ratiocinations, its tea-parties in suave South Audley Street . . .' and contrasted them with the excited discussions of Verlaine and his fellow poets in small cafés. 'The discussions in obscure cafés regenerated, remade French poetry; but the Poets' Club! . . . the Poets' Club is death.'[8]

Out of the lively argument that ensued grew a firm friendship between Flint and Hulme. Flint at that time was already an advocate of *vers libre* and was said to be a man who knew more of contemporary French poetry than anyone else in London. Hulme, although never completely severing his connection with the Poets' Club, now formed a new (unnamed) society in conjunction with Flint. Its first meeting was held on 25 March 1909 in the Eiffel Tower, a restaurant in Soho; and its members included F. W. Tancred, Joseph Campbell, Florence Farr and Edward Storer. They met on Thursday evenings, and their talk was of the state of contemporary poetry and how it might be replaced 'by *vers libre*, by the Japanese tanka and haikai . . .' and by '. . . poems in a sacred Hebrew form.' In all this, wrote Flint later, 'Hulme was the ringleader. He insisted too on absolutely accurate presentation and no verbiage... There was also a lot of talk and practice among us, Storer leading it chiefly, of what we called the Image. We were very much influenced by Modern French Symbolist poetry.'[9] Edward Storer had already written in an essay at the end of his book of poems, *Mirrors of Illusion*: 'There is no absolute virtue in iambic pentameters as such ... however well done they may be. There is no immediate virtue in rhythm even. These things are merely means to an end. Judged by themselves, they are monstrosities of childish virtuosity and needless iteration.' *Vers libre* was already taking hold and Hulme was to echo Storer's feelings in a lecture on modern poetry delivered in 1914: '[This] is my objection to metre, that it enables people to write verse with no poetic inspiration, and whose mind [*sic*] is not stored with new images.'[10]

It was to this Hulme-Flint group that Ezra Pound, then aged twenty-four and only recently arrived in London, was introduced in April 1909 – a month after its foundation. But it is interesting to note that he too was already thinking along lines similar to those of this group, with their 'absolutely accurate presentation and no verbiage', when he wrote to William Carlos Williams, the American poet, on 21 October 1908, of his 'ultimate attainments of poesy' as:

1. To paint the thing as I see it.
2. Beauty.
3. Freedom from didacticism.
4. It is only good manners if you repeat a few other men to at least do it better or more briefly. Utter originality is of course out of the question.[11]

In 1911 Hilda Doolittle (twenty-six and already calling herself H.D.) arrived in London and re-met Ezra Pound – she had been engaged to him in America but her father had put his foot down firmly, calling Pound '... nothing but a nomad!'[12] She also met in London another poet, Richard Aldington, twenty years old and soon to be her husband. He had in common with H.D. a tremendous interest in Greek poetry which was to prove a strong driving force in both their poetry. This was the year too when Harriet Monroe (art critic of the Chicago *Tribune*) founded the magazine *Poetry* and appointed Ezra Pound its foreign representative. Hulme had in the meantime attended a philosophical congress at Bologna at which Henri Bergson discussed 'the image' and Pound almost certainly attended Hulme's subsequent lectures on Bergson.

The time was right for the formation of a movement along the lines of the discussions of Hulme and his 'Eiffel Tower' group. After all they had an example of a successful revolutionary movement of a similar kind in the French Symbolists; they had an energetic and sympathetic poet in Ezra Pound; and Ford Madox Ford tells us that he too was 'hammering ceaselessly' at Pound and Hulme that 'poetic ideas are best expressed by the rendering of concrete objects'.[13]

Pound was looking around for good poetry to send to Harriet Monroe for *Poetry* and found it in the recent poems of H.D. and Richard Aldington. They used to meet in a tea-shop in Kensington and give poems to Pound for criticism. It was at such a meeting in the spring of 1912 that Pound told the two poets (much to their surprise) that they were IMAGISTES – the use of the rather precious French version of the word, implying perhaps their connection with the modern French School, was soon abandoned for the English style.

Richard Aldington says in his autobiography that it was probably the first time he had heard that 'Pickwickian word'. He believed, he tells us, that the name took Pound's fancy and that 'he kept it *in petto* for the right occasion';[14] and for Pound this was the 'right occasion'. He said he was going to send the six poems – three by Aldington: 'Choricos', 'To a Greek Marble' and 'Au Vieux Jardin'; and three by H.D.: 'Hermes of the Ways', 'Priapus' and 'Epigram' – to the magazine *Poetry*. He was so taken with H.D.'s that he insisted they be signed: 'H.D. Imagiste.' No one else would look at their poems at that time and so they agreed. Pound wrote to Harriet Monroe in October: 'I've had luck again, and am sending you some *modern* stuff by an American. I say modern, for it is in the laconic speech of the Imagistes, even if the subject is classic ... This is the sort of American stuff that I can show here and in Paris without its being ridiculed. Objective – no slither; direct – no excessive use of adjectives, no metaphors that won't permit examination. It's straight talk, straight as the Greek!'[15]

In that same month Pound's own volume of poems called *Ripostes* appeared, and as an appendix he had included what he called 'The Complete Poetical Works of T. E. Hulme' with a prefatory note in which the word Imagiste was used in print for the first time: 'As for the future, Les Imagistes, the descendants of the forgotten school of 1909, have that in their keeping.' It was these poems of Hulme that led T. S. Eliot to speak of Hulme in 1924 as 'the author of two or three of the most beautiful short poems in the language.'[16]

The three poems by Adlington duly appeared in *Poetry* for November 1912 together with a biographical note explaining: 'Mr Richard Aldington is a young English poet, one of the "Imagistes", a group of ardent Hellenists who are pursuing interesting experiments in *vers libre*; trying to attain in English certain subleties of cadence of the kind which Mallarmé and his followers have studied in French.' H.D.'s three poems appeared in January 1913 (signed H.D. Imagiste) with a longer note saying: '... The youngest school here that has the nerve to call itself a school is that of the Imagistes ... one of their watchwords is Precision, and they are in opposition to the numerous and unassembled writers who busy themselves with dull and interminable effusions ...'

It was inevitable that questions would be asked and explanations given. And in *Poetry* for March 1913 we find the first statements of policy – 'Imagisme' by F. S. Flint; and 'A Few Don'ts by an Imagiste' by Ezra Pound (see Appendix, pages 129-34) in which he defines the 'Image' as 'that which presents an intellectual and emotional complex in an instant of time'. Flint's note on Imagisme includes three rules:

1. Direct treatment of the 'thing' whether subjective or objective.

2. To use absolutely no word that did not contribute to presentation.

3. As regarding rhythm: to compose in sequence of the musical phrase not in sequence of a metronome.

A letter from Pound as late as 26 September 1927 states that the 'test is in the second of the three clauses of the first manifesto'.[17]

From Pound's 'Don'ts' a few examples are sufficient to show the general line of argument:

'Use no superfluous word, no adjective which does not reveal something...

'Go in fear of abstractions ...

'Use either no ornament or good ornament ...

'Don't chop your stuff into separate iambs. Don't make each line stop dead at the end, and then begin every next line with a heave...'

The inevitable step after this was a full-scale launching of the movement with an anthology, with H.D. and Richard Aldington as the centre-pieces. Pound had wanted to promote their work – later he confessed that the name Imagisme 'was invented to launch H.D. and Aldington before either had enough stuff for a volume'.[17]

He selected ten poems by Aldington, seven by H.D., included six of his own which were the nearest to imagist principles, and filled out the rest of the book with contemporaries who were sympathetic. These were F. S. Flint, Skipwith Cannell, Amy Lowell, William Carlos Williams, James Joyce, Ford Madox Hueffer, Allen Upward and John Cournos. The anthology was published in March 1914 under the title of *Des Imagistes*. In an article in *The Little Review* (an American periodical) for July 1914 Charles Ashleigh, discussing this anthology, remembered that Richard Aldington had said: '... that five of those whose poems are there included are not true Imagists. These are Cournos, Hueffer, Upward, Joyce, and Cannell ... I [i.e. Charles Ashleigh] maintain that, all unconsciously, the publishers ... have dealt a blow to sectarian Imagism by including these non-Imagist poems in their anthology.'[18] Some of these however I include in this anthology since they do to a certain extent reveal a tendency towards Imagism among poets who did not understand the term; and there is historical interest in the fact that Pound chose them to represent the movement.

Des Imagistes was badly received both in Britain and America; and in London many returned their copies to the Poetry Bookshop, who published it. There was no preface to explain the new techniques, and the title seemed too precious and cryptic. Two of Flint's best-known poems, 'London' and 'The Swan', were in the anthology. Both had already appeared in *Poetry* for July 1913, and they are particularly interesting in that we have the originals from which these imagist versions stemmed (see Appendix, pages 148-9). 'The Swan' was to appear again very soon in a controversy that arose between Pound and Flint over the latter's interpretation of Imagism and his view of the founding of the movement in his 'History of Imagism' in the special imagist issue of the periodical *Egoist* (1 May 1915). Pound wrote to Flint saying that he thought his History 'bullshit'. Flint replied: 'I am glad you consider it the product of a *bull*: you might have considered it the product of a cow, or, worse still of a bullock . . .' So began bitter enmity between the two which lasted until 1921 – the whole affair is admirably documented elsewhere[19] and indicates clearly the tensions that led to inevitable break-up. Pound was upset by Flint's stress on Storer's pre-imagism, and called it 'custard' which could in no way have led to H.D.'s 'Hellenic hardness'. He points to the difference between Flint's original 'A Swan Song' and the imagist version. Flint's reply is significant: '. . . As to the difference between Imagism of 1909 and 1913 the illustration of my "Swan" chosen by you is a bad one, because the real difference between the two poems is one of form merely, and I am not sure that, apart from one or two weaknesses of style (I was less mature then than now) the earlier version (that is so far as the first strophe is conceived: the rest was deleted) is not the better imagist poem. In any case I do not think much light was vouchsafed me on the evening you mention, when you jabbed at the poem with the stub of a pencil . . .'[20] Earlier in the letter we get an even more personal view of Pound: 'As to energy . . . you deserve all credit for what you have done . . . But where you have failed, my dear Ezra . . . is in your personal relationships; and I repeat, we all regret it . . . You have not been a good comrade, voilà!' Pound kept to his view long after the quarrel was ended. Even in 1927 he wrote of Flint as really an 'impressionist'.[17]

In January 1915 Pound had already written to Harriet Monroe telling her that he was not having anything to do with a forthcoming anthology entitled *Some Imagist Poets*. And in a letter to her a few weeks later Pound repeats (see Appendix, page 141): 'Poetry must be *as well written as prose* . . . Objectivity and again objectivity . . . Language is made out of concrete things. General expressions in non-concrete terms are a laziness . . . The only adjective that is worth using is the adjective that is essential to the sense of the passage, not the frill adjective . . .'[21]

Pound was quite clear about this; and when he sensed a slackening of dedication in the others, he was perhaps wise to depart for the more intensive Vorticism, which was a stricter form of Imagism. It was gaining ground in its opposition to Futurism, which Pound described as a kind of 'accelerated impressionism . . . a *spreading* or surface art'.[22] He was already involved in the Vorticist magazine *Blast*, and in September 1914 he had written an article on 'Vorticism' in the *Fortnightly Review*:

There is a sort of poetry where music, sheer melody, seems as if it were just bursting into speech.

There is another sort of poetry where painting or sculpture seems as it were 'just coming over into speech'.

The first sort of poetry has long been called 'lyric' . . . The other sort of poetry is as old as the lyric and as honourable, but until recently, no one named it. Ibycus and Liu Ch'e presented the 'Image'. Dante is a great poet by reason of this faculty, and Milton is a wind-bag because of his lack of it. The 'Image' is the furthest possible remove from rhetoric. Rhetoric is the art of dressing up some unimportant matter so as to fool the audience for the time being . . . As a 'critical' movement, the 'Imagism' of 1912 to '14 set out 'to bring poetry up to the level of prose'.[23]

But more significant is his differentiation in the same article between 'Imagisme' and 'Symbolisme':

The symbolists dealt in 'association', that is, in a sort of allusion, almost of allegory. They degraded the symbol to the status of a word, they made it a form of metronomy. One can be grossly 'symbolic' for example, by using the term 'cross' to mean 'trial'. The symbolist's *symbols* have a fixed value, like numbers in arithmetic, like 1, 2 and 7. The imagist's images have a variable significance like the signs a, b, and x in algebra . . . the author must use his *image* because he sees it or feels it, *not* because he thinks he can use it to back up some creed or some system of ethics or economics . . .[24]

This is the heart of Imagism; and perhaps at that time Pound was the only one of the group to understand fully its implications.

His departure from the movement was made more inevitable by the intervention of Amy Lowell. H.D. had tried to smooth over the Flint – Pound controversy. But there were many reasons why Pound should not stay with the movement and already Amy Lowell had moved in on the promotion side. She had arrived in England from Boston in 1914 eager to be the high-powered saleswoman of Imagism to America. She had met the Imagists already and discussed the contemporary French literary scene with them, and now was intent on substituting 'pure democracy' among the Imagists for Pound's 'despotism'.[25] She had an excess of money and character. She was known to have two passions in life – Keats and cigars – and now she had settled into her accustomed suite at the Berkeley Hotel with its view across Piccadilly to Green Park, and no doubt was travelling London in her familiar mulberry-coloured car with two chauffeurs in matching livery.[26]

She proposed a 'Boston Tea Party'[27] for Pound, to establish her democracy. The Imagists were to publish quietly as a group of friends with similar tendencies rather than with dogmatic principles. Each poet was to choose for himself what he considered best in his year's output and an anthology – *Some Imagist Poets* – would appear annually. Poets were to appear in alphabetical order in the volumes, and Amy Lowell undertook all the practical work to get the books published in Boston and London. Pound refused to contribute on those terms; he feared the return of flabbiness into the poems. He warned her in a letter (1 August 1914): 'I should like the name 'Imagisme' to retain some sort of meaning. It stands, or I should like it to stand, for hard light, clear edges. I can not trust any democratized committee to maintain that standard. Some will be splay-footed and some sentimental.'[28] It is interesting here to note that even at the time of *Des Imagistes*, Aldington and H.D. were worried about Amy Lowell's first book of poems, *A Dome of Many-Coloured Glass* (1912), which they had thought 'fluid, fruity, facile stuff'.[29]

Pound added in a letter to Amy Lowell on 12 August 1914: 'I think your idea most excellent, only I think your annual anthology should be called *Vers Libre* or something of that sort . . . If you want to drag in the word Imagisme you can use a subtitle "an anthology devoted to Imagisme, *vers libre* and modern movements in verse" or something of that sort. I think that will be perfectly fair to everyone.'[30]

She still insisted on the title *Some Imagist Poets*. And when an advertisement of her book of poems, *Sword Blades and Poppy Seed*, carried the words: '... *The foremost member of the "Imagists" – a group of poets that includes William Butler Yeats, Ezra Pound, Ford Madox Hueffer* ...' Pound's only answer, in the face of the publishers' 'arrant charlatanism', was: 'I think you had better cease referring to yourself as an Imagiste.'[31]

She continued; and brought out the first of her anthologies in April 1915, followed by two others in 1916 and 1917. Those for 1915 and 1916 contained explanatory prefaces (see Appendix, pages 134-40). These were of course statements of intent rather than assessments of accomplishment, and the second of them was noted in *The Times Literary Supplement* (4 January 1917) as '... a preface written with commendable sense and restraint, and is particularly of interest in its defence of *vers libre*'. Pound was right: the tendency was away from hardness and towards *vers libre* which was a form they had accepted from the beginning but in which it was all too easy to be 'splay-footed'. A review of the 1917 anthology in *Poetry* for March 1918, confirms this: 'Unfortunately, imagism has now come to mean almost any kind of poetry written in unrhymed irregular verse, and "the image" – referred solely to the visual sense – is taken to mean some sort of pictorial impression.'

This doesn't mean, however, that all the poems in the Amy Lowell anthologies were 'flabby'; indeed many of the best Imagist poems are to be found in them, and the 1915 anthology is certainly better than Pound's *Des Imagistes* – in 1914, of course, there was little material from which to make a choice. Pound summed up his feelings about the 1915-17 period when he called it the period of 'Amy-gism' and all that that word implied; and he wrote in August 1917: 'I don't think any of these people have gone on; have invented much since the first *Des Imagistes* anthology.'[32]

Letters from H.D. to Flint during this period imply that she and Richard Aldington did most of the planning for the 1915 anthology:

'We have a new plan for the anthology', she wrote, 'and want – need – to talk it over with you before writing Amy . . .' (19 December 1914). And another letter (22 March 1916), again to Flint, indicates further misunderstandings and the separation of Pound from the others: 'E.P. wrote: I think he expects to get R's [*Aldington's*] job on the *Egoist* (in *strict confidence*) – But we did not answer his charming Macheavellian [*sic*] note!'[33] There are also hints in these letters of a growing rift between Amy Lowell and the London Imagists, and H.D.'s attempts to repair damage caused by Amy Lowell's headstrong methods.*

After the 1917 anthology Amy Lowell wrote in her *Tendencies in Modern American Poetry*: 'There will be no more volumes of *Some Imagist Poets*. The collection has done its work. These three little books are the germ, the nucleus, of the school; its spreading out, its amplifications, must be sought in the unpublished work of the individual members of the group.'[34]

In spite of Pound's statement to the contrary, Amy Lowell did extend the range of Imagism – for good or ill. She introduced a new form – Polyphonic Prose, an extension of *vers libre*. John Gould Fletcher, the American poet, writing of *vers libre*, said: '. . . a critical examination of the work of the best of these young poets – Aldington, H.D., Flint, Pound – proves that their attempt has not been altogether successful . . . Intense and concise grasp of substance is not enough; the ear instinctively demands that this bare skeleton be clothed fittingly with all the beautiful and subtle orchestral qualities of assonance, alliteration, rhyme, and return.

'This orchestral quality Miss Lowell has developed to the utmost. Therefore it seems fitting that a new name should be given to these poems of hers . . . The title that fits them best is that of Polyphonic Prose.'[35] An example of this style is the extract on page 88 entitled 'Spring Day' taken from the 1916 anthology.

* Cyrena N. Pondrom, the editor of these *Selected Letters from H.D. to F. S. Flint* in *Contemporary Literature* (Autumn 1969) refers to Charles Norman's *Ezra Pound* (New York, Macmillan, 1960), pages 154–5, with its suggestion that one of the sources of conflict between Pound and Amy Lowell was his anger when Amy Lowell said she was unable to put up money to enable him to take over as editor of the *Mercure de France*.

Amy Lowell ascribed the form to Paul Fort – his *Ballades françaises* employed rhyme and verse-form but were printed as prose – but it was she who linked it with Imagism. She adopted Flint's phrase 'unrhymed cadence' too, as an appropriate English equivalent of *vers libre*; and brought John Gould Fletcher (another expatriate) into the movement on his passionate support for *vers libre*.

He also experimented in Polyphonic Prose and carried the 'orchestral qualities' into his verse too. He attempted with some success to express what he termed 'the emotional relations that exist between form, colour and sound'.[36] His 'Blue Symphony' in eleven movements was included in *Some Imagist Poets 1915*. Pound said later that Fletcher never 'accepted the imagist program'.[37]

But the outstanding acquisition to the group for Amy Lowell was D. H. Lawrence. By the time she met him, he was sufficiently well-known to be a 'prize'. He was already contributing to the Georgian anthologies, but Amy Lowell asked him for material. He refused. She insisted that he was an Imagist, and quoted back at him his own poetry:

> The morning breaks like a pomegranate
> In a shining crack of red ...[38]

Lawrence was too much of an individualist to be taken in by this, or by a group manifesto; but he had no cogent objection and so he gave in. Aldington says in his autobiography: 'As anyone can see from his *Collected Poems* even Lawrence was for a time influenced by H.D.; so that his work fitted in perfectly.'[39] But Pound wrote: 'I will go so far as to say that Lawrence was never an Imagist. He was an *Amy*gist.'[40]

Certainly he was influenced by them – what sensitive poet in close contact with them could fail to be? – but his was too passionate a view to give direct objective hardness to his poetry. He was perhaps attracted more to the rebellious side of the movement; also he shared with John Gould Fletcher an admiration of Whitman, and with F. S. Flint a background of poverty (Flint used the word 'fleabitten' of his own upbringing). H.D.'s autobiographical novel *Bid Me To Live* (1963) gives a thinly disguised and fine portrait of Lawrence; and his emotional nearness to the group is evident. He was certainly an advocate of *vers libre*: '... the direct utterance from the instant whole man.'[41] But a critic noticed of his work: '[He] is a fine poet, but he employs similes – or rather the employment of similes is too essential a part of his method to let his work, for the time being, have much claim to the epithets "restrained" or "exact" . . .'[42] – epithets necessary to true imagist writing.

Through all this period of the anthologies the chief organ of the Imagists was the periodical the *Egoist: An Individualist Review*. *The English Review* had been founded in 1909 by Ford Madox Hueffer who was sympathetic to Pound's ideas, and he published him together with Flint and Lawrence. But when the magazine changed hands in 1910 there was only *Poetry Review*, a monthly, left, and its successor, *Poetry and Drama*, which appeared quarterly, published by Harold Monro of the Poetry Bookshop. This in turn was suspended in 1914 and replaced by *The Chapbook: A Monthly Miscellany* until 1923. These were all of help in one way or another to the Imagists; and of course there were *Poetry* and *The Little Review* (an American periodical run by Margaret C. Anderson). But the Imagists needed their own outlet. Pound had his eye on a periodical owned by Harriet Shaw Weaver, and edited by her in conjunction with Dora Marsden in 1913. It was called *The New Freewoman: An Individualist Review*; and by 1 January 1914 the ladies had agreed to the Imagists moving in, had renamed the periodical *Egoist*, and had allowed it to be entirely devoted to literary matters on condition that Dora Marsden should always contribute the leading article – on feminism. Richard Aldington was its first imagist editor (together with Dora Marsden and Harriet Weaver in turn); but by 1916 H.D. and Richard Aldington together were the assistant editors; and when Aldington went to the war in 1917, T. S. Eliot joined H.D. on the editorial board. The periodical was suspended in December 1919.

T. S. Eliot, since his arrival in England in 1914, had always stayed on the borders of the imagist movement. He was never an orthodox Imagist, but in many ways he took naturally to some of their theories although developing them along his own lines. Even before he came to England, his 1909–11 poems – 'Preludes', 'The Love Song of J. Alfred Prufrock', and 'Rhapsody on a Windy Night' (published later) were imagistic in their tendency towards depersonalizing the poetic voice – a recurrent idea in his writings: 'The progress of an artist is a continual self-sacrifice, a continual extinction of personality.'[43] He had also been studying Bergson in Paris at that time; and it was Ezra Pound and John Gould Fletcher who persuaded Harriet Monroe to publish 'Prufrock' in *Poetry* (1915). The Egoist Press brought out his *Prufrock and Other Observations* in 1917.*

Among other writers to appear in the *Egoist* were Wyndham Lewis, Marianne Moore, William Carlos Williams, Rémy de Gourmont, and James Joyce, whose *Portrait of the Artist as a Young Man* ran as a serial. They wanted to serialize Joyce's *Ulysses* but could find no printer who would undertake it. The Egoist Press eventually published the book in 1922.

The Imagists as a group movement were at an end in 1917, except for one further anthology of which Richard Aldington tells in his autobiography:

In 1929 my modernistic friend, Walter Lowenfels, suggested to me in Paris that I ought to get out another imagist anthology. Of course I knew Walter thought the Imagists were as dead as Shelley, and that the suggestion was ironical. By way of snubbing him I promptly took a taxi to the cable office, and as I had just published a successful novel I had no difficulty in selling the non-existent anthology to London and New York within two days ... I got to work, Ford and H.D. laboured nobly, and the *Imagist Anthology 1930*, contained poems by everyone who had contributed (including James Joyce and Carlos Williams) except poor Amy who was dead, Skipwith Cannell whom we couldn't trace, and Ezra who was sulky.[44]

This 1930 anthology throws the whole subject of Imagism back into the melting-pot, since few of the poems, except perhaps H.D.'s and William Carlos Williams's, are what one had thought Imagism to be. There is a need to return to T. E. Hulme and Ezra Pound and basic principles. The foreword to the 1930 anthology by Glenn Hughes however contains a statement important to any assessment of the Imagists as a group: 'None of them was interested in a movement for

*For discussion of a theory that T. S. Eliot's poem 'The Death of St Narcissus' was influenced by Pound's 'A Girl' and Hulme's 'Conversion', see Grover Smith: *T. S. Eliot's Poetry and Plays* (University of Chicago Press, 1956), p. 34.

its own sake; each of them was interested in being a poet. Having certain common beliefs, and being faced in common with certain prejudices, they joined forces for a time and marched against the enemy, waving a single banner. That they won their fight is incontestable. And having won it they threw the banner away, broke ranks, and became frankly what they had been all the time: individual artists.'[45]

When looking for first principles, one could go as far as Robert Duncan, the American poet, does in his *H.D. Book*, and say that 'the main drive of the Imagists away from the specially "poetic" diction of the nineteenth century toward the syntax and rhythms of common daily speech was that of Dante in his *De Vulgari Eloquentia* . . .'[46] Or one could come nearer in time, to Schopenhauer with his declaration that if a man ceases to consider the where, the when, the why, and the whither of things and looks simply and solely at the *what*: 'if further, he does not allow abstract thought, the concept of reason . . . but instead of all this gives the whole power of his mind to perception . . . the quiet contemplation of the natural object actually present, whether a landscape, a tree, a mountain, a building, or whatever it may be; inasmuch as he *loses* himself in this object . . . then that which is so known is no longer the particular thing as such; but is the Idea, the eternal form . . .'[47] Or, since Schopenhauer was one of the principal influences on Bergson, and Bergson on Hulme, we might go straight to Hulme – always remembering however not to exaggerate his influence on the Imagists. They were already thinking and working along his lines independently; and this drew them together in the first place.

T. E. Hulme was a man who assimilated material quickly, and, never a truly original thinker, was able and ready to turn it easily to his own ends. He absorbed, for instance, Jules de Gaultier's evaluation of sculptured poetry,[48] Henri Bergson's theories of interpenetration,[49] and large slices of Théodule Ribot[50] and Rémy de Gourmont.[51]* Here we should not forget Pound who must receive his due, in that

*See Wallace Martin, 'The Sources of the Imagist Aesthetic' P.M.L.A. (Vol. 85 No. 2, March 1970) pp. 196–204, for an extended discussion of this topic.

he also had read Gourmont before compiling the first imagist manifesto, and could have arrived at his theories independently.[52]

Hulme's theories are complicated, repetitive, and frequently muddled, but certain ideas stand out as clear pointers towards Imagism.

First he distinguishes between the romantic and the classical and says that the root of all romanticism is that man feels 'the individual is an infinite reservoir; and if you can so rearrange society by the destruction of oppressive order then these possibilities will have a chance and you will get Progress.

'One can define the classical quite clearly as the exact opposite to this. Man is an extraordinarily fixed and limited animal whose nature is absolutely constant. It is only by tradition and organization that anything decent can be got out of him.'[53] Hulme attacks in particular the sentimentality into which the romantic disposition often fell. 'Verse to them always means a bringing in of some of the emotions that are grouped round the word infinite.'[54] 'I object to the sloppiness which doesn't consider that a poem is a poem unless it is moaning or whining about something or other.'[55] The poetry of the immediate past was for Hulme the depth of this romantic decadence: 'We shall not get any new efflorescence of verse until we get a new technique, a new convention, to turn ourselves loose in.'[56] He then prophesied 'a period of dry, hard, classical verse is coming'.[57] He pinned faith on the classical poet who 'never forgets this finiteness, this limit of man. He remembers always he is mixed up with earth. He may jump, but he always returns back; he never flies away into the circumambient gas'.[58]

From Bergson Hulme took the distinction of *intellect* and *intuition*. Intellect merely analyses, while intuition is a placing of the artist 'back within an object by a kind of sympathy and breaking down ... the barrier that space puts between him and his model'.[59] There is a clarifying passage in Hulme's own translation of Bergson's *An Introduction to Metaphysics*: 'Many diverse images, borrowed from very different orders of things, may, by the convergence of their action, direct consciousness to the precise point where there is a certain intuition to be seized.'[60]

Hulme concluded that prose is the vehicle for intellect: poetry for intuition.

From Rémy de Gourmont's *Problème du Style*** Hulme took and developed the idea that language is always on the point of extinction and that it must be constantly injected with fresh metaphors. 'One might say that images are born in poetry. They are used in prose and finally die a long lingering death in journalists' English. Now this process is very rapid, so that a poet must continually be creating new images.'[61] 'The direct language is poetry, it is direct because it deals in images. The indirect is prose, because it uses images that have died and become figures of speech.'[62]

Hulme saw (with the aid of Flint) how the French Symbolists, who had dominated French poetry between 1880 and 1900, had freed French poetry from the tyranny of conventional form; and how, under the pioneering of Gustave Kahn, such poets as Laforgue (later to influence Eliot so much) had developed the technique of *vers libre*.

Hulme's aim then was to revitalize the language, to get away from vagueness and the infinite of the 'circumambient gas' by means of precise definition, and to centre on *intuition*. A complete freshness of approach is needed: 'We must judge the world from the status of animals, leaving out "Truth" etc. . . . Animals are in the same state that men were before symbolic language was invented.'[63] Hulme insisted that if the sentence or phrase were regarded as the unit of meaning instead of the word, the relation between words within that sentence or phrase would yield a spark of fresh analogies revealing a particular, singular, intuition.[64] If this was to work, poetry must rid itself of romanticism and become impersonal, hard – as Eliot said: 'The emotion of art is impersonal.'[65] This attitude of the impersonal, the objective, led naturally to another characteristic of the Imagists – their dislike of the moralizing tone of the Victorians.

A look at one of the finest imagist poems will help towards a

*For a discussion of whether it was Gourmont or Ribot who influenced Hulme see Wallace Martin in P.M.L.A. March 1970, pp. 202–3; and Alun R. Jones: 'Imagism: A Unity of Gesture' in *American Poetry*, Stratford-on-Avon Studies No. 7 (Arnold, 1965).

definition. H.D.'s 'Oread' appeared in *Some Imagist Poets 1915* and was used by Pound (in his definition of Vorticism) as the ultimate in Imagism:

> Whirl up, sea –
> Whirl your pointed pines,
> Splash your great pines
> On our rocks,
> Hurl your green over us,
> Cover us with your pools of fir.

'It is petty poetry,' wrote Harold Monro in the special Imagist number of the *Egoist*. 'It can be said in one minute before lunch. Such images should appear by the dozen in poetry. Such reticence denotes either poverty of imagination or needlessly excessive restraint.'[66] And Conrad Aiken wrote of the whole group: 'Of organic *movement* there is practically none.'[67]

But these two critics have come with preconceptions. The Imagists were taking a *fresh* look. They didn't regard themselves as revolutionaries – the word was given to them by their critics – and in fact Flint said: 'Of course, we have never, as Imagists, claimed to have invented the moon. We do not pretend that our ideas are original.'[68] Thus many of the points to be made about 'Oread' are bound to take the form of negatives if we look at it in the context of its contemporaries.

There are no similes in the poem, no symbols – presentation rather than representation; no moralizing tone; no reflection on human experience (a danger here perhaps in lack of human concern); no striving for the spiritual; no fixed metre or rhyme – but a rhythm organic to the image itself; no narrative – it needs none; no vagueness of abstractions – it would destroy the image. There is however a strong sense of the abstract caught within the concrete; and no form but the poem itself. It is not forced to take upon itself a fixed shape, except that of the image in isolation ecstatically held. It is not merely description, but evocation; and to use Pound's words: 'The gulf between evocation and description . . . is the unbridgeable difference between genius and talent.'[69]

There was a reply to Harold Monro's 'petty poetry' criticism, by May Sinclair, in the next issue of the *Egoist*. 'The Victorian poets are

Protestants. For them the bread and the wine are symbols of Reality, the body and the blood. They are given "in remembrance". The sacrament is incomplete. The Imagists are Catholic; they believe in Transubstantiation ... For them the bread and the wine are the body and blood. They are given. The thing is done. *Ite Missa est.*'[70] She also gives several examples of Imagism from the past. Dante's souls of the damned falling like leaves for instance ...

> Come d'autunno si levan le foglie
> L'una appresso dell'altra, infin che'l ramo
> Rende alle terra tutte le sue spoglie.

'... it makes no difference,' she says, 'whether he says they *are* leaves or only *like* leaves. The flying leaves are the perfect image of the damned souls. Only the identity is incomplete.' While in Suckling's simile:

> Her feet beneath her petticoat,
> Like little mice, stole in and out ...

the mice are not the perfect image of his lady's feet, 'only a partial and imperfect image of their appearance'.

In 'Oread' we are given an evocation by means of an analogy taken to the point of perfect fusion, taken in its most direct form, allowing not so much each word its full weight as the *whole* poem. 'Thought', says Hulme, 'is prior to language and consists in the simultaneous presentation of two different images.'[71] 'The form of a poem is shaped by the intention.'[72] It is the *whole* poem that is experienced, not a beautiful line, a clever rhyme, or a nicely turned simile. The poem has become the unit of meaning and not the word; thus each individual word can remain simple and unpretentious. It is the relation *between* the words that contains the meaning. It is at this point that the image becomes not merely a vehicle for transcribing a sensation but presents the sensation itself. In 'Oread', the sea *is* the pine-wood: the pine-wood *is* the sea: and the mountain nymph of the title becomes fused with the two. The wind surrounds all three. The analogy sparks off the poem at the point of fusion. Further images, further organic movement is unnecessary. 'The point of Imagisme', says Pound, 'is that it does not use images as ornaments. The image itself is the speech. The image is the word beyond formulated language.'[73] On those terms it is no wonder that H.D. was so often praised as the 'perfect imagist' and Flint wrote of her: 'The form of her poems seems to me to be so inevitable that those who cannot accept it had better pass on.'[74] 'Oread' reminds one of those still-lifes of Cézanne where the folds of a cloth begin to take on the characteristics of his beloved Mt Saint-Victoire; or, taken further, one can think of the gradual but startling simplifications that took place in the paintings of Matisse, until there were only shapes of colour left on the canvas to vibrate at the point of their juxtaposition. Pound perhaps best summed up this kind of poem when writing of his own 'In a Station of the Metro':

> The apparition of these faces in the crowd;
> Petals on a wet, black bough.

'In a poem of this sort one is trying to record the precise instant when a thing outward and objective transforms itself, or darts into a thing inward and subjective.'[75]

All this is a counsel of perfection, and for obvious reasons such marble purity as that of 'Oread', or of many of H.D.'s other poems, is rare and restricted in poetic range. We cannot consistently demand such intensity and concentration from the Imagists. For many of the group, simply to present objectively and artistically the materials of life which aroused their emotions was enough.

Some of the faults of Imagism are evident: the limitations of *true* Imagism, and the excessive freedom outside that purity of form and texture. But perhaps the most dangerous fault of all was pointed out by John Gould Fletcher: 'It was the fault of imagism never to let its devotees draw clear conclusions about life and to force the poet to state too much and to deduce too little – to lead its disciples too often into a barren aestheticism which was, and is, empty of content ... Poetry merely descriptive of nature as such, however vivid, no longer seems to me enough; there has to be added to it the human judgement, the human evaluation.'[76]

A list of a few titles of critical essays during the period of the imagist anthologies indicates shock or enthusiasm, mingled with misunderstanding: 'The Spiritual Dangers of Writing Vers Libre';[77] 'The Piano and Imagism';[78] 'Vers Libre and Advertising':[79] 'Poetry Versus Imagism';[80] 'The New Naiveté';[81] plus a later crop of amusing parodies under the heading 'Pathology des Dommagistes' (1921)[82] (see Appendix, page 151).

Indignation melted eventually in some cases into genuine enthusiasm, and in others into acceptance and assimilation; but not before there had been a notable attack by Professor John Livingstone Lowes in *Nation* (1916);[83] and rhetoric nearing violence from Professor William Ellery Leonard in four articles in the *Chicago Evening Post* (1915).[84] There was also an expected controversy about *vers libre* and the point where poetry becomes prose and vice versa. The best appraisal of this was to be seen in the columns of the *New Statesman* in March 1917,[85] when T. S. Eliot took a stand against not so much the practice of *vers libre* as the definition of it: '*Vers libre* does not exist, for there is only good verse, bad verse and chaos.' John Gould Fletcher retaliated: 'Does [Mr Eliot's statement] affect the fact that once a thing is deliberately and constantly practised a new name had to be found for it? Can Mr Eliot suggest a more appropriate name than *vers libre*'?[86] The whole problem of the prose-poem is brought in: true Imagism is forgotten again. A similar argument in America grew between Professor John Livingstone Lowes and Amy Lowell. He declared: 'Miss Lowell's free verse may be written as very beautiful prose; George Meredith's prose may be written as very beautiful free verse. Which is which?'[87] She replied: '... there is no difference ... Whether a thing is written as prose or verse is immaterial.'[88] By 1918 *Poetry* was able to say: 'Free verse is now accepted in good society, where rhymed verse is even considered a little shabby and old-fashioned.'[89]

But all this was a discussion forgetting the real point of Imagism and it is encouraging to read the critics who were more worried about the heart of the matter: '[Some Imagists] were so terrified at Cosmicism that they ran into a kind of Microcosmicism, and found their greatest emotional excitement in everything that seemed intensely small.'[90] This of course Hulme would have approved with his own 'It is essential to prove that beauty may be in small, dry things.'[91] But Leonard again counteracts this: 'Imagists, doubtless, hear things more wonderful than Beethoven's symphonies in the buzz of the mosquito on the flats back of Chicago, and they whiff more than all the perfumes of Arabia in the summer steam of a Jersey dunghill.'[92]

In 1915 Hueffer thought that only H.D. and F. S. Flint had the really exquisite sense of words '... Mr John Gould Fletcher, Mr Aldington, and Miss Lowell are all too preoccupied with themselves and their emotions to be called Imagists';[93] while Harriet Monroe, in 1914, was anxious to call Emily Dickinson an 'unconscious and uncatalogued *Imagiste*'.[94]

Perhaps the best contemporary assessment came from *The Times Literary Supplement* (11 January 1917):

Imagist poetry fills us with hope; even when it is not very good in itself, it seems to promise a form in which very good poetry could be written ... The worst of the old forms of verse now is that so often they seem to impose their own moods on those who use them ... [The Imagist] can let the form follow the mood instead of imposing on it ... The value of his form is in its power of acceptance, not of rejection; and so, if it is to justify itself, it must be rich, not empty. He cannot supersede the pretty nothings of the past with ugly nothings ... If Imagist poetry can open our literature to all things that a poet would say and think naturally, and if at the same time it can give him a form in which he will say them far better than in ordinary thought or speech, then it will have justified itself.

The most telling test of a movement is its staying power or the strength of its influence; and in the case of the imagist movement these are evident but confused. When Pound wrote that Imagism was a point on the curve of his development, 'some people remained at that point, I moved on'; and William Carlos Williams in his *Autobiography* says, 'We had had "Imagism" ... which ran quickly out ...'[95]; they were perhaps being too self-conscious in their rejection of something already assimilated, as was Debussy in his rejection of Wagner when he wrote *Pelléas et Mélisande*. Certainly it is easy to take from (say) Carlos Williams's letters to Denise Levertov isolated quotations and declare them totally imagist. 'Cut and cut again', he writes, 'whatever you write – while you leave by your art no trace of your cutting – and the final utterance will remain packed with what you have to say,'[96] (23 August 1954). Or again: 'The test of the artist is to be able to revise without showing a seam ... It is quite often no more than knowing what to *cut* ...' (13 June 1956). These could easily have been written by Pound or Hulme in 1914; and one is reminded of a story told by Harold Monro in his *Some Contemporary Poets* of a young countryman of Pound's arriving in England, and visiting him with specimens of his work. Pound sat for a long time in deep consideration of a certain poem and at length, glancing up, remarked: 'It took you 97 words to do it; I find it could have been managed in 56.' But there is nothing specifically 'imagist' in this cutting – nothing new. Yet we must also remember that that is precisely what the Imagists kept pointing out: 'These principles are not new; they have fallen into desuetude. They are the essentials of all great poetry.'[97] This 'ridding the field of verbiage',[98] this 'greatest admiration for the past, and humility towards it',[99] was not the only influential part of their work. There are still poets working within the tensions of the short imagistic poem with considerable success. There is no sense of staleness or pastiche in the poems of Ian Hamilton, for instance, or Colin Falck – no sense of a failure to move on. They are not as depersonalized as the imagist poems of H.D. nor do they have her hard, marble quality; but they have much positive austerity that will not admit the sentimental. They have what Aldington said of H.D.'s poetry ... 'a kind of accurate mystery'.[100] Imagistic ideas have been totally assimilated into a thoroughly modern outlook.

Other more experimental developments can be traced to Imagism. In February 1931 *Poetry* brought out a special objectivist number edited by Louis Zukofsky who included 'The Botticellian Trees' by Carlos Williams as an objectivist poem and one by Charles Reznikoff which could well have appeared in *this* anthology of imagist poetry;

> From my window I could not see the moon,
> And yet it was shining:
>
> The yard among the houses –
> Snow upon it –
> An oblong in the darkness.

Zukofsky stated as required reading: Pound's *XXX Cantos*; Carlos Williams's *Spring and All*; T. S. Eliot's *The Waste Land* and *Marina*; Marianne Moore's *Observations*; E. E. Cummings', *Is 5*; Wallace Stevens's, *Harmonium*, among others; and declared, 'In contemporary writing the poems of Ezra Pound alone possess objectivication to a most constant degree; his objects are musical shapes.' An objectivist anthology came out in 1932, again edited by Zukofsky, including work by Basil Bunting, Robert McAlmon, George Oppen, Carl Rakos, Kenneth Rexroth, Charles Reznikoff and William Carlos Williams. Ezra Pound is represented by his 'Yittischer Charleston'; and Eliot by 'Marina'.

The connection with the original Imagists is clear and made more evident by a statement such as that of the American poet, Jack Spicer, in *Letter to Lorca* (1957):

'I would like to make poems out of real objects ...* I would like to point to the real, disclose it, to make a poem that has no sound in it but the pointing of a finger ... The poem is a collage of the real ... *Things do not connect; they correspond* [my italics]. That tree you saw in Spain is a tree I could never have seen in California, that lemon has a different smell and a different taste, BUT the answer is this – every place and every time has a real object to *cor-respond* [his italics] with your real object – *that lemon may become this lemon, or it may even become this piece of seaweed, or this particular color of gray in this ocean. One does not need to imagine that lemon; one needs to discover it*' [my italics].[101]

Or again from Wallace Stevens's *Adagia* (a notebook written between 1930 and 1955): 'Poetry has to be something more than a conception of the mind. It has to be a revelation of nature. Conceptions are artificial. Perceptions are essential.'[102] This recalls Pound's: 'The image is not an idea.' (1914) As with the Imagists, authentic feeling is the result of a direct perception of, or contact with, the real. Or as Carlos Williams puts it: 'no ideas but in things.'[103]

*It is interesting to note in this context that Norman N. Holland, writing in the *International Journal of Psycho-Analysis* No. 50 (1969) of 'Freud and H.D.', with special reference to her *Tribute to Freud* and her description of Freud's study, speaks of her 'remarkable ability (and defensive need) to recreate the touch and feel of various objects; she is much less able to recreate people ... H.D. was above all a poet of the thingness of things.' (p. 310)

There is a clear line of influence too through Carlos Williams to Charles Olson, and on to Levertov, Creeley, and Robert Duncan. And there is also E. E. Cummings, whose typographical prosody is a by-product of Imagism, particularly when one remembers Hulme's words that 'this new verse resembles sculpture rather than music. It builds up a plastic image which it hands over to the reader'.[104] Cummings's shaped poems are intended to point the total syntax – the shape *is* the syntax. Hulme's dictum that we must regard the phrase rather than the word as the unit of meaning had led both to the focusing of the eye on the poem as a whole, and to the possibility of highlighting details by means of *vers libre*. It was line length or word isolation rather than the syntax that pointed the image or the cadence – often there is broken syntax in imagistic writing.

This visual element almost certainly influenced another *Egoist* poet, Marianne Moore, although she does not admit it. The dry richness of her syllabic verse is the kind of hard classical discipline too of which Hulme would have approved. 'One writes,' she says, 'because one has a burning desire to objectify what is indispensable to one's happiness to express . . .,'[105] and this objectification is clear when one *sees* the precision of her lines on the page. 'Precision,' she also wrote, 'economy of statement, logic employed to ends that are disinterested . . . liberate the imagination.'

The other side of objectivism is shown by T. S. Eliot in his theory of the Objective Correlative: 'The only way of expressing emotion in the form of art is by finding an "objective correlative"; in other words, a set of objects, a situation, a chain of events which shall be the formula of that *particular* emotion; such that when the external facts, which must terminate in sensory experience, are given, the emotion is immediately evoked.'[106] This is very near to true imagist practice, but here Eliot's image is not so much presented as *used*; this perhaps is where he parted company with the Imagists and was at heart always more of a symbolist.

But more important for this anthology is the way the Imagists themselves introduced an element of mysticism into their poetry (particularly H.D.), and how different this was from the turn-of-the-

38

century-circumambient-gas kind of spirituality against which they fought.

John Gould Fletcher for instance in such poems as numbers XIV and XVIII from *Irradiations* (pages 73–4) implies a theory of inter-penetration of subject and object to the point of total empathy. The Bergsonian theory of the artist 'placing himself back within the object by a kind of sympathy'[107] is reiterated in Fletcher's preface to his *Goblins and Pagodas*,[108] where he is discussing how various poets would treat a book on his desk: '[I would] link up my personality and the personality of the book and make each a part of the other. In this way I should strive to evoke a soul out of this piece of inani-mate matter, a something characteristic and structural inherent in this organic form which is friendly to me and responds to my mood.

'This method is not new ... Professor Fenellosa ... calls this doctrine of the interpenetration of man and inanimate nature, the cardinal doctrine of Zen Buddhism.'

Richard Aldington too in the introduction to his *Complete Poems* wrote: '... By the sense of mystery I understand the experience of certain places and times when one's whole nature seems to be in touch with a presence, a genius loci, a potency.'[109]

Pound had defined the Image as 'that which presents an intellectual and emotional complex in an instant of time'; and yet failed at that point to enlarge convincingly on the meaning of an 'intellectual and emotional complex', except to say that it was in the 'technical sense employed by the new psychologists such as Hart'. In his essay *The Conception of the Subconscious* Hart describes Freud's dream image as being conceived as constellated by a large number of unconscious complexes. As a result of the combination and interaction of these complexes a single image emerges into consciousness.[110] This idea of a 'complex' was expanded by Pound in his *As For Imagisme*:

The Image can be of two sorts. It can arise within the mind. It is then 'subjective'. External causes play upon the mind perhaps; if so, they are drawn into the mind, fused, transmitted, and emerge in an Image unlike themselves. Secondly, the Image can be 'objective'. Emotion seizing upon some external scene or action carries it in fact to the mind;

and that vortex purges it of all save the essential or dominant or dramatic qualities, and it emerges like the external original.

In either case the Image is more than an idea. It is a vortex or cluster of fused ideas and is endowed with energy. If it does not fulfil these specifications, it is not what I mean by an Image.[111]

This admission of the subconscious element is frequent in Pound's attempt at a definition of the Image – of his own 'Metro' poem he had written that it was 'the precise instant when a thing outward and objective transforms itself, darts into a thing inward and subjective'.[112]

The period of the Imagists was also the period of the Subconscious-Seekers – whether of myth or mind: Frazer, Jessie Weston, Freud, Jung, Croce, Whitehead.* All of them contributed to make the complex deep enough to reach the very Word, the Logos, the Divine – to be held in the word, the phrase, the analogy, the image. This is the hard centre (however subjective it might prove) and not the circumambient gas of the pseudo-romantics.

By its very nature Imagism could not contain narrative – and narrative was not essential to this inward progression. Indeed the great poems to come after the Imagist period – Eliot's *The Waste Land* and *Four Quartets*; Pound's *Cantos*; Carlos Williams's *Paterson* – contain no defining narrative. There is a feeling of a missing narrative in *The Waste Land* (drastically cut by Eliot with, significantly, Pound's help), and *Four Quartets* have an inward progression where narrative would be out of place; and there is no *end* to the *Cantos* or *Paterson*.

The same applies to H.D.'s war trilogy, arguably her greatest work. Written during the Second World War – *The Walls Do Not Fall*, *Tribute to the Angels*, and *The Flowering of the Rod* – it stands in Robert Duncan's estimation with 'Pound's *Cantos*, Eliot's *Four Quartets*, and William Carlos Williams's *Paterson* as a major work of the Imagist genius in its full'.[113] Its search for the Word at the still centre implies a quest similar to Eliot's, and its parallel metaphors are true to H.D.'s methods. And even when she adopts a looser form, as she does in the war trilogy, she still does not impose a narrative

*For longer discussion of this point see Robert Duncan's review of *Selected Poems of H.D.* in *Poetry* (Chicago), January 1958.

pattern. I have included a brief extract from this major work in this anthology; but so few lines cannot even begin to indicate the depth of understanding contained in the work as a whole. It is a pity that too often an extract from the war trilogy has to stand so near her early imagist work – it is different in scope and range of sympathy and should be seen in its entirety as distinct in its achievement from her early work. The same is true of her last major work *Helen in Egypt*.

When H.D. translated Euripides' *Ion* she interspersed the various scenes with prose comment; and time and again these notes proceed from a characteristic imagistic hardness of description into the abstract or spiritual. Of Kreousa, she says: 'Kreousa has the inhumanity of a meteor sunk under the sea . . . here is rock, air, wings, loneliness . . . A woman is about to step out of stone, in the manner of a later Rodin.'[114] In her *Tribute to Freud* too, the hallucination that came to her on the island of Corfu in 1920 seems to be an attempt to make the abstract concrete; and with Freud's help later she is able to find a universal from that concrete form of vision.

A further aspect of the problem of imagistic writing in contemporary poetry is the poem of length. Imagist poetry is concise, tight and precise, with no narrative. How does it cope with a subject of considerable complexity? Eliot supplies a clue in his preface to his translation of St.-John Perse's *Anabase*: 'Any obscurity of the poem, on first readings, is due to the suppression of "links in the chain", of explanatory and connecting matter, and not to incoherence or to love of cryptogram. The justification of such abbreviation or method is that the sequence of images coincides and concentrates into one impression of barbaric civilization. The reader has to allow the images to fall into his memory without questioning the reasonableness of each at the moment; so that, at the end, a total effect is produced. Such selection of a sequence of images and ideas has nothing chaotic about it. There is a logic of the imagination as well as a logic of concepts.'[115]

How easily could this stand as an introduction to the imagistic 'lists', the precise images flashed on to the screen of Pound's later *Cantos*, unrelated by grammatical connections; and the introduction of Chinese ideograms – the ultimate hard image for Pound. Here there is tremendous faith on Pound's part in the instinctive synthesis and the truth that emerges from it. It is the peak of a style which Amy Lowell attempted (in a rather insipid form) in her prose-poem *Can Grande's Castle*, with its sequence of tableaux; and has found root again in Charles Olson's theories of Projective Verse: 'ONE PERCEPTION MUST IMMEDIATELY AND DIRECTLY LEAD TO A FURTHER PERCEPTION ... always, always one perception must must must MOVE INSTANTER, ON ANOTHER!'[116]

H.D. used a similar but more considered technique in longer works – her trilogy novel *Palimpsest* is, as the title implies, an exemplum of this method. Here the sharp juxtaposing or overlaying of three analogous tales brings a new dimension to the novel: 'Something compounded like faces seen one on top of another,'[117] she writes; and in her novel *Bid Me To Live*: 'They seemed to be superimposed on one another like a stack of photographic negatives.'[118] James Joyce applies a similar technique in his fiction, and it is clear why the Imagists chose to serialize him in the *Egoist*.

It is at the point of meeting of analogous images that the potency lies: 'Oread' is alive *in toto*; and Carlos Williams, although writing specifically of Marianne Moore, put his finger on a universal truth:

A course in mathematics would not be wasted on a poet or reader of poetry if he remember no more from it than the geometric principle of the intersection of loci: from all angles lines converging and crossing establish points. He might carry it further and say in his imagination that apprehension perforates at places, through to understanding – as white is at the intersection of blue and green and yellow and red. It is this white light that is the background of all good work.[119]

Or as H.D. wrote in the second part of her war trilogy, *Tribute To The Angels*, section XLIII:

> And the point in the spectrum
> where all lights become one,
>
> is white and white is not no-colour,
> as we were told as children,
>
> but all-colour;
> where the flames mingle

and the wings meet, when we gain
the arc of perfection,

we are satisfied, we are happy,
we begin again;

'Life, for eternal us, is now'[120] wrote E. E. Cummings introducing
his own poems, and it is for this that the first Imagists ought to be
remembered – the 'reconciliation of the finite and the infinite' to be
found in their 'insistence on concrete exactness, on freedom in the
choice of subject, on concentration as of the very essence of poetry'
and for their 'pioneering work, too, in the discovery of new forms
and rhythms'.[121]

THE CHOICE OF POEMS

This anthology attempts to be an historical account of the movement,
and contains the original lineation and titles of the poems taken from
the imagist anthologies, even where (particularly in the case of
D. H. Lawrence) the poems were substantially altered later. Marianne
Moore appears in the central section with poems from the *Egoist*,
and she has asked me to point out particularly that the versions that
appeared in that periodical contained errors which are corrected in
this anthology; they are not later revisions. Her poem 'You are Like
the Realistic Product of an Idealistic Search for Gold at the Foot of
the Rainbow' she later retitled 'To a Chameleon'. I am most grateful
for her help in this matter. In attempting to give a full picture of the
movement I have included some poems which do not appear to be
central to the imagist ideal, but illustrate variations from it and the
broadness with which it was interpreted. I have omitted quotation
from Ezra Pound's 'Cantos' in the post-Imagist section, both because
the work does not lend itself to selected quotation and because it is
readily available elsewhere.

THE PRE-IMAGISM IMAGISTS

EDWARD STORER

Image

Forsaken lovers,
Burning to a chaste white moon,
Upon strange pyres of loneliness and drought.

Street Magic

One night I saw a theatre,
                    Faint with foamy sweet,
And crinkled loveliness
Warm in the street's cold side.

Beautiful Despair

I look at the moon,
And the frail silver of the climbing stars;
I look, dear, at you,
And I cast my verses away.

T. E. HULME

Autumn

A touch of cold in the Autumn night –
I walked abroad,
And saw the ruddy moon lean over a hedge
Like a red-faced farmer.
I did not stop to speak, but nodded,
And round about were the wistful stars
With white faces like town children.

Above the Dock

Above the quiet dock in midnight,
Tangled in the tall mast's corded height,
Hangs the moon. What seemed so far away
Is but a child's balloon, forgotten after play.

Conversion

Light-hearted I walked into the valley wood
In the time of hyacinths,
Till beauty like a scented cloth
Cast over, stifled me. I was bound
Motionless and faint of breath
By loveliness that is her own eunuch.

Now pass I to the final river
Ignominiously, in a sack, without sound,
As any peeping Turk to the Bosphorus.

The Sunset

A coryphée, covetous of applause,
Loth to leave the stage,
With final diablerie, poises high her toe,
Displays scarlet lingerie of carmin'd clouds,
Amid the hostile murmurs of the stalls.

The Man in the Crow's Nest
(Look-out Man)

Strange to me, sounds the wind that blows
By the masthead, in the lonely night
Maybe 'tis the sea whistling – feigning joy
To hide its fright
Like a village boy
That trembling past the churchyard goes.

Images

Old houses were scaffolding once
                    and workmen whistling.
            *
Her skirt lifted as a dark mist
From the columns of amethyst.
            *
Sounds fluttered,
                like bats in the dusk.
            *
The flounced edge of skirt,
                recoiling like waves off a cliff.

THE PERIOD OF THE ANTHOLOGIES
1914–17

Poems that appeared
in the anthologies are noted:
Des Imagistes 1914 – D.I.
Some Imagist Poets 1915/16/17 – S.I.P.1915/16/17.

RICHARD ALDINGTON

Au Vieux Jardin
(D.I.)

I have sat here happy in the gardens,
Watching the still pool and the reeds
And the dark clouds
Which the wind of the upper air
Tore like the green leafy boughs
Of the divers-hued trees of late summer;
But though I greatly delight
In these and the water lilies,
That which sets me nighest to weeping
Is the rose and white colour of the smooth flag-stones,
And the pale yellow grasses
Among them.

Epigrams
(S.I.P. 1915)

New Love

She has new leaves
After her dead flowers,
Like the little almond tree
Which the frost hurt.

October

The beech-leaves are silver
For lack of the tree's blood.

At your kiss my lips
Become like the autumn beech-leaves.

A Girl

You were that clear Sicilian fluting
That pains our thought even now.
You were the notes
Of cold fantastic grief
Some few found beautiful.

Amalfi

We will come down to you,
O very deep sea,
And drift upon your pale green waves
Like scattered petals.

We will come down to you from the hills,
From the scented lemon-groves,
From the hot sun
We will come down,
O Thalassa,
And drift upon
Your pale green waves
Like petals.

Images

1

Like a gondola of green scented fruits
Drifting along the dark canals of Venice,
You, O exquisite one,
Have entered my desolate city.

2

The blue smoke leaps
Like swirling clouds of birds vanishing.

So my love leaps towards you
Vanishes and is renewed.

3

A rose-yellow moon in a pale sky
When the sunset is faint vermilion
On the mist among the tree-boughs
Are you to me.

4

As a young beech-tree on the edge of a forest
Stands still in the evening,
Then shudders through all its leaves in the light air
And seems to fear the stars –
So are you still and so tremble.

5

The red deer are high on the mountain,
They are beyond the last pine-trees.
And my desires have run with them.

6

The flower which the wind has shaken
Is soon filled again with rain:
So does my heart fill slowly with tears
Until you return.

Sunsets
(S.I.P. 1916)

The white body of the evening
Is torn into scarlet,
Slashed and gouged and seared
Into crimson,
And hung ironically
With garlands of mist.

And the wind
Blowing over London from Flanders
Has a bitter taste.

To a Greek Marble
(D.I.)

Πότνια, πότνια,
White grave goddess,
Pity my sadness,
O silence of Paros.

I am not of these about thy feet,
These garments and decorum;
I am thy brother,
Thy lover of aforetime crying to thee,
And thou hearest me not.

I have whispered thee in thy solitudes
Of our loves in Phrygia,
The far ecstasy of burning noons
When the fragile pipes
Ceased in the cypress shade,
And the brown fingers of the shepherd
Moved over slim shoulders;
And only the cicada sang.

I have told thee of the hills
And the lisp of reeds
And the sun upon thy breasts,

And thou hearest me not,
Πότνια, πότνια,
Thou hearest me not.

Picket

Dusk and deep silence . . .

Three soldiers huddled on a bench
Over a red-hot brazier,
And a fourth who stands apart
Watching the cold rainy dawn.

Then the familiar sound of birds –
Clear cock-crow, caw of rooks,
Frail pipe of linnet, the 'ting! ting!' of chaffinches,
And over all the lark
Outpiercing even the robin . . .

Wearily the sentry moves
Muttering the one word: 'Peace'.

Insouciance

In and out of the dreary trenches
Trudging cheerily under the stars
I make for myself little poems
Delicate as a flock of doves.

They fly away like white-winged doves.

Living Sepulchres

One frosty night when the guns were still
I leaned against the trench
Making for myself *hokku*
Of the moon and flowers and of the snow.

But the ghostly scurrying of huge rats
Swollen with feeding upon men's flesh
Filled me with shrinking dread.

Evening

The chimneys, rank on rank,
Cut the clear sky;
The moon,
With a rag of gauze about her loins
Poses among them, an awkward Venus –

And here am I looking wantonly at her
Over the kitchen sink.

Nocturnes
(D.I.)

V

I am weary with love, and thy lips
Are night-born poppies.
Give me therefore thy lips
That I may know sleep.

VI

I am weary with longing,
I am faint with love;
For upon my head has the moonlight
Fallen
As a sword.

JOHN COURNOS

The Rose
(after K. Tetmaier)
(D.I.)

I remember a day when I stood on the sea shore at Nice, holding a scarlet rose in my hands.

The calm sea, caressed by the sun, was brightly garmented in blue, veiled in gold, and violet, verging on silver.

Gently the waves lapped the shore, and scattering into pearls, emeralds and opals, hastened towards my feet with a monotonous, rhythmical sound, like the prolonged note of a single harp-string.

High in the clear, blue-golden sky hung the great, burning disc of the sun.

White seagulls hovered above the waves, now barely touching them with their snow-white breasts, now rising anew into the heights, like butterflies over the green meadows ...

Far in the east, a ship, trailing its smoke, glided slowly from sight as though it had foundered in the waste.

I threw the rose into the sea, and watched it, caught in the wave, receding, red on the snow-white foam, paler on the emerald wave.

And the sea continued to return it to me, again and again, at last no longer a flower, but strewn petals on restless water.

So with the heart, and with all proud things. In the end nothing remains but a handful of petals of what was once a proud flower ...

H.D.

Epigram
(after the Greek)
(D.I.)

The golden one is gone from the banquets;
She, beloved of Atimetus,
The swallow, the bright Homonoea;
Gone the dear chatterer.

Priapus
Keeper-of-Orchards
(D.I.)

I saw the first pear
As it fell.
The honey-seeking, golden-banded,
The yellow swarm
Was not more fleet than I,
(Spare us from loveliness!)
And I fell prostrate,
Crying.
Thou hast flayed us with thy blossoms;
Spare us the beauty
Of fruit-trees!

The honey-seeking
Paused not.
The air thundered their song,
And I alone was prostrate.

61

O rough-hewn
God of the orchard,
I bring thee an offering;
Do thou, alone unbeautiful
(Son of the god),
Spare us from loveliness.

The fallen hazel-nuts,
Stripped late their green sheaths,
The grapes, red-purple,
Their berries
Dripping with wine,
Pomegranates already broken,
And shrunken fig,
And quinces untouched,
I bring thee as offering.

Oread
(S.I.P. 1915)

Whirl up, sea –
Whirl your pointed pines,
Splash your great pines
On our rocks,
Hurl your green over us,
Cover us with your pools of fir.

Evening

The light passes
from ridge to ridge,
from flower to flower –
the hypaticas, wide-spread
under the light
grow faint –
the petals reach inward,
the blue tips bend
toward the bluer heart
and the flowers are lost.

The cornel-buds are still white,
but shadows dart
from the cornel-roots –
black creeps from root to root,
each leaf
cuts another leaf on the grass,
shadow seeks shadow,
then both leaf
and leaf-shadow are lost.

Sitalkas
(D.I.)

Thou art come at length
More beautiful
Than any cool god
In a chamber under
Lycia's far coast,
Than any high god
Who touches us not
Here in the seeded grass.
Aye, than Argestes
Scattering the broken leaves.

Hermes of the Ways
(D.I.)

I

The hard sand breaks,
And the grains of it
Are clear as wine.

Far off over the leagues of it,
The wind,
Playing on the wide shore,
Piles little ridges,
And the great waves
Break over it.

But more than the many-foamed ways
Of the sea,
I know him
Of the triple path-ways,
Hermes,
Who awaiteth.

Dubious,
Facing three ways,
Welcoming wayfarers,
He whom the sea-orchard
Shelters from the west,
From the east
Weathers sea-wind;
Fronts the great dunes.

Wind rushes
Over the dunes,
And the coarse, salt-crusted grass
Answers.

Heu,
It whips round my ankles!

II

Small is
This white stream,
Flowing below ground
From the poplar-shaded hill,
But the water is sweet.

Apples on the small trees
Are hard,
Too small,
Too late ripened
By a desperate sun
That struggles through sea-mist.

The boughs of the trees
Are twisted
By many bafflings;
Twisted are
The small-leafed boughs.
But the shadow of them
Is not the shadow of the mast head
Nor of the torn sails.

Hermes, Hermes,
The great sea foamed,
Gnashed its teeth about me;
But you have waited,
Where sea-grass tangles with
Shore-grass.

The Garden
(S.I.P. 1915)

I

You are clear,
O rose, cut in rock,
hard as the descent of hail.

I could scrape the colour
from the petal,
like spilt dye from a rock.

If I could break you
I could break a tree.

If I could stir
I could break a tree,
I could break you.

II

O wind,
rend open the heat,
cut apart the heat,
rend it sideways.

Fruit can not drop
through this thick air:
fruit can not fall into heat
that presses up and blunts
the points of pears
and rounds the grapes.

Cut the heat,
plough through it,
turning it on either side
of your path.

The Pool
(S.I.P. 1915)

Are you alive?
I touch you.
You quiver like a sea-fish.
I cover you with my net.
What are you – banded one?

Sea Rose
(S.I.P. 1915)

Rose, harsh rose,
marred and with stint of petals,
meagre flower, thin,
sparse of leaf,

more precious
than a wet rose,
single on a stem –
you are caught in the drift.

Stunted, with small leaf,
you are flung on the sands,
you are lifted
in the crisp sand
that drives in the wind.

Can the spice-rose
drip such acrid fragrance
hardened in a leaf?

From Euripides' *Iphegeneia in Aulis*

Chorus of the Women of Chalkis (extract)

3

A flash –
Achilles passed across the beach.
(He is the sea-woman's child
Chiron instructed.)

Achilles had strapped the wind
About his ankles,
He brushed rocks
The waves had flung.
He ran in armour.

He led the four-yoked chariot
He had challenged to the foot-race.
Emelos steered
And touched each horse with pointed goad.

I saw the horses:
Each beautiful head was clamped with gold.

Silver streaked the centre horses.
They were fastened to the pole.
The outriders swayed to the road-stead.
Colour spread up from ankle and steel-hoof.
Bronze flashed.

And Achilles, set with brass,
Bent forward,
Level with the chariot-rail.

4

If a god should stand here
He could not speak
At the sight of ships
Circled with ships.

This beauty is too much
For any woman.
It is burnt across my eyes.

The line is an ivory-horn.
The Myrmidons in fifty quivering ships
Are stationed on the right.

These are Achilles' ships.
On the prow of each
A goddess sheds gold:
Sea-spirits are cut in tiers of gold.

JOHN GOULD FLETCHER

The Skaters
To A.D.R.
(S.I.P. 1916)

Black swallows swooping or gliding
In a flurry of entangled loops and curves;
The skaters skim over the frozen river.
And the grinding click of their skates as they
    impinge upon the surface,
Is like the brushing together of thin wing-tips
    of silver.

The Unquiet Street
(S.I.P. 1916)

By day and night this street is not still;
Omnibuses with red tail-lamps,
Taxicabs with shiny eyes,
Rumble, shunning its ugliness.
It is corrugated with wheel-ruts,
It is dented and pockmarked with traffic,
It has no time for sleep.
It heaves its old scarred countenance
Skyward between the buildings
And never says a word.

On rainy nights
It dully gleams
Like the cold tarnished scales of a snake:
And over it hang arc-lamps
Blue-white death-lilies on black stems.

70

Dawn

(S.I.P. 1917)

Above the east horizon,
The great red flower of the dawn
Opens slowly, petal by petal:
The trees emerge from darkness
With ghostly silver leaves,
Dew-powdered.
Now consciousness emerges
Reluctantly out of tides of sleep;
Finding with cold surprise
No strange new thing to match its dreams,
But merely the familiar shapes
Of bedpost, window-pane and wall.

Within the city,
The streets which were the last to fall to sleep,
Hold yet stale fragments of the night.
Sleep oozes out of stagnant ash-barrels,
Sleep drowses over litter in the streets.
Sleep nods upon the milkcans by back doors.
And, in shut rooms,
Behind the lowered window-blinds,
Drawn white faces unwittingly flout the day.

But, at the edges of the city,
Sleep is already washed away;
Light filters through the moist green leaves,
It runs into the cups of flowers,
It leaps in sparks through drops of dew,
It whirls against the window-panes
With waking birds;
Blinds are rolled up and chimneys smoke,
Feet clatter past on silent paths,
And down white vanishing ways of steel,

A dozen railway trains converge
Upon night's stronghold.

From *Irradiations*

VII

Flickering of incessant rain
On flashing pavements:
Sudden scurry of umbrellas:
Bending, recurved blossoms of the storm.

The winds came clanging and clattering
From long white highroads whipping in ribbons up
    summits:
They strew upon the city gusty wafts of apple-blossom,
And the rustling of innumerable translucent leaves.

Uneven tinkling, the lazy rain
Dripping from the eaves.

IX

The houses of the city no longer hum and play:
They lie like careless drowsy giants, dumb, estranged.

One presses to his breast his toy, a lighted pane:
One stirs uneasily: one is cold in death.

And the late moon, fearfully peering over an immense
    shoulder,
Sees, in the shadow below, the unpeopled hush of a street.

X

The trees, like great jade elephants,
Chained, stamp and shake 'neath the gadflies of the breeze;
The trees lunge and plunge, unruly elephants:
The clouds are their crimson howdah-canopies,
The sunlight glints like the golden robe of a Shah.
Would I were tossed on the wrinkled backs of those trees.

XIV

Brown bed of earth, still fresh and warm with love,
Now hold me tight:
Broad field of sky, where the clouds laughing move,
Fill up my pores with light:
You trees now talk to me, chatter and scold or weep,
Or drowsing stand,
You winds, now play with me, you wild things creep,
You boulders, bruise my hand!
I now am yours and you are mine: it matters not
What Gods herein I see:
You grow in me, I am rooted to this spot,
We drink and pass the cup, immortally.

XVII

The wind that drives the fine dry sand
Across the strand:
The sand wind spinning arabesques
With a wrinkled hand.

Labyrinths of shifting sand,
The dancing dunes!

I will arise and run with the sand,
And gather it greedily in my hand:
I will wriggle like a long yellow snake over the beaches.
I will lie curled up, sleeping.
And the wind shall chase me
Far inland.

My breath is the music of the mad wind;
Shrill piping, stamping of drunken feet,
The fluttering, tattered broidery flung
Over the dunes' steep escarpments.

The fine dry sand that whistles
Down the long low beaches.

XVIII

Blue, brown, blue: sky, sand, sea:
I swell to your immensity.
I will run over the endless beach,
I will shout to the breaking spray,
I will touch the sky with my fingers,
My happiness is like this sand:
I let it run out of my hand.

EPILOGUE

The barking of little dogs in the night is more
    remembered than the shining of the stars:
Only those who watch for long may see the moon rise:
And they are mad ever after and go with blind eyes
Nosing hungrily in the gutter for the scraps that
    men throw to the dogs;
Few heed their babblings.

F. S. FLINT

London
(D.I.)
See Appendix, page 148

London, my beautiful,
it is not the sunset
nor the pale green sky
shimmering through the curtain
of the silver birch,
not the quietness;
it is not the hopping
of birds
upon the lawn,
nor the darkness
stealing over all things
that moves me.

But as the moon creeps slowly
over the tree-tops
among the stars,
I think of her
and the glow her passing
sheds on men.

London, my beautiful,
I will climb
into the branches
to the moonlit tree-tops,
that my blood may be cooled
by the wind.

Beggar

In the gutter
piping his sadness
an old man stands,
bent and shrivelled,
beard draggled,
eyes dead.

Huddled and mean,
shivering in threadbare clothes –
winds beat him,
hunger bites him,
forlorn, a whistle in his hands,
piping.

Hark! the strange quality
of his sorrowful music,
wind from an empty belly
wrought magically
into the wind –

pattern of silver on bronze.

November

What is eternal of you
I saw
in both your eyes.

You were among the apple branches;
the sun shone, and it was November.

Sun and apples and laughter
and love
we gathered, you and I.

And the birds were singing.

76

Cones
(S.I.P. 1916)

The blue mist of after-rain
fills all the trees;

the sunlight gilds the tops
of the poplar spires, far off,
behind the houses.

Here a branch sways
and there
                    a sparrow twitters.

The curtain's hem, rose-embroidered,
flutters, and half reveals
a burnt-red chimney pot.

The quiet in the room
bears patiently
a footfall on the street.

Searchlight
(S.I.P. 1917)

There has been no sound of guns,
no roar of exploding bombs;
but the darkness has an edge
that grits the nerves of the sleeper.

He awakens;
nothing disturbs the stillness,
save perhaps the light, slow flap,
once only, of the curtain
dim in the darkness.

Yet there is something else
that drags him from his bed;
and he stands in the darkness
with his feet cold against the floor
and the cold air round his ankles.
He does not know why,
but he goes to the window and sees
a beam of light, miles high,
dividing the night into two before him,
still, stark and throbbing.

The houses and gardens beneath
lie under the snow
quiet and tinged with purple.

There has been no sound of guns,
no roar of exploding bombs;
only that watchfulness hidden among the snow-covered houses,
and that great beam thrusting back into heaven
the light taken from it.

Soldiers
To R.A.
(S.I.P. 1917)

Brother,
I saw you on a muddy road
in France
pass by with your battalion,
rifle at the slope, full marching order,
arm swinging;
and I stood at ease,
folding my hands over my rifle,
with my battalion.
You passed me by, and our eyes met.
We had not seen each other since the days
we climbed the Devon hills together:
our eyes met, startled;
and, because the order was Silence,
we dared not speak.

O face of my friend,
alone distinct of all that company,
you went on, you went on,
into the darkness;
and I sit here at my table,
holding back my tears,
with my jaw set and my teeth clenched,
knowing I shall not be
even so near you as I saw you
in my dream.

The Swan
(D.I.)
See Appendix, page 149

Under the lily shadow
and the gold
and the blue and mauve
that the whin and the lilac
pour down on the water,
the fishes quiver.

Over the green cold leaves
and the rippled silver
and the tarnished copper
of its neck and beak,
toward the deep black water
beneath the arches
the swan floats slowly.

Into the dark of the arch the swan floats
and into the black depth of my sorrow
it bears a white rose of flame.

FORD MADOX FORD

From *Antwerp*

VI

This is Charing Cross;
It is midnight;
There is a great crowd
And no light.
A great crowd, all black that hardly whispers aloud.
Surely, that is a dead woman – a dead mother!
She has a dead face;
She is dressed all in black;
She wanders to the bookstall and back,
At the back of the crowd;
And back again and again back,
She sways and wanders.

This is Charing Cross;
It is one o'clock.
There is still a great cloud, and very little light;
Immense shafts of shadows over the black crowd
That hardly whispers aloud . . .
And now! . . . That is another dead mother,
And there is another and another and another . . .
And little children, all in black,
All with dead faces, waiting in all the waiting-places,
Wandering from the doors of the waiting-room
In the dim gloom.

These are the women of Flanders.
They await the lost.
They await the lost that shall never leave the dock;

They await the lost that shall never again come by the train
To the embraces of all these women with dead faces;
They await the lost who lie dead in trench and barrier and foss,
In the dark of the night.
This is Charing Cross; it is past one of the clock;
There is very little light.

There is so much pain.

JAMES JOYCE

I Hear an Army
(D.I.)

I hear an army charging upon the land,
And the thunder of horses plunging; foam about their knees:
Arrogant, in black armour, behind them stand,
Disdaining the reins, with fluttering whips, the Charioteers.

They cry into the night their battle name:
I moan in sleep when I hear afar their whirling laughter.
They cleave the gloom of dreams, a blinding flame,
Clanging, clanging upon the heart as upon an anvil.

They come shaking in triumph their long grey hair:
They come out of the sea and run shouting by the shore.
My heart, have you no wisdom thus to despair?
My love, my love, my love, why have you left me alone?

D. H. LAWRENCE

Green
(S.I.P. 1915)

The sky was apple-green,
The sky was green wine held up in the sun,
The moon was a golden petal between.

She opened her eyes, and green
They shone, clear like flowers undone,
For the first time, now for the first time seen.

Illicit
(S.I.P. 1915)

In front of the sombre mountains, a faint, lost ribbon
    of rainbow,
And between us and it, the thunder;
And down below, in the green wheat, the labourers
Stand like dark stumps, still in the green wheat.

You are near to me, and your naked feet in their sandals,
And through the scent of the balcony's naked timber
I distinguish the scent of your hair; so now the limber
Lightning falls from heaven.

Adown the pale-green, glacier-river floats
A dark boat through the gloom – and whither?
The thunder roars. But still we have each other.
The naked lightnings in the heaven dither
And disappear. What have we but each other?
The boat has gone.

At the Window
(S.I.P. 1916)

The pine-trees bend to listen to the autumn wind as it mutters
Something which sets the black poplars ashake with hysterical
  laughter;
While slowly the house of day is closing its eastern shutters.

Further down the valley the clustered tombstones recede
Winding about their dimness the mists' grey cerements, after
The street-lamps in the twilight have suddenly started to bleed.

The leaves fly over the window and whisper a word as they
  pass
To the face that leans from the darkness, intent, with two eyes
  of darkness
That watch forever earnestly from behind the window glass.

Brooding Grief
(S.I.P. 1916)

A yellow leaf from the darkness
Hops like a frog before me –
– Why should I start and stand still?

I was watching the woman that bore me
Stretched in the brindled darkness
Of the sick-room, rigid with will
To die –
And the quick leaf tore me
Back to this rainy swill
Of leaves and lamps and traffic mingled before me.

Autumn Rain

The plane leaves
fall black and wet
on the lawn;

the cloud sheaves
in heaven's fields set
droop and are drawn

in falling seeds of rain;
the seed of heaven
on my face

falling – I hear again
like echoes even
that softly pace

heaven's muffled floor,
the winds that tread
out all the grain

of tears, the store
harvested
in the sheaves of pain

caught up aloft:
the sheaves of dead
men that are slain

now winnowed soft
on the floor of heaven;
manna invisible

of all the pain
here to us given;
finely divisible
falling as rain.

AMY LOWELL

In a Garden
(D.I.)

Gushing from the mouths of stone men
To spread at ease under the sky
In granite-lipped basins,
Where iris dabble their feet
And rustle to a passing wind,
The water fills the garden with its rushing,
In the midst of the quiet of close-clipped lawns.

Damp smell the ferns in tunnels of stone,
Where trickle and plash the fountains,
Marble fountains, yellowed with much water.

Splashing down moss-tarnished steps
It falls, the water;
And the air is throbbing with it;
With its gurgling and running;
With its leaping, and deep, cool murmur.

And I wished for night and you.
I wanted to see you in the swimming-pool,
White and shining in the silver-flecked water.
While the moon rode over the garden,
High in the arch of night,
And the scent of the lilacs was heavy with stillness.

Night and the water, and you in your whiteness, bathing!

Spring Day
(extract)
(S.I.P. 1916)

Midday and Afternoon

Swirl of crowded streets. Shock and recoil of traffic. The stock-still brick façade of an old church, against which the waves of people lurch and withdraw. Flare of sunshine down side-streets. Eddies of light in the windows of chemists' shops, with their blue, gold, purple jars, darting colours far into the crowd. Loud bangs and tremors, murmurings out of high windows, whirling of machine belts, blurring of horses and motors. A quick spin and shudder of brakes on an electric car, and the jar of a church bell knocking against the metal blue of the sky. I am a piece of the town, a bit of blown dust, thrust along with the crowd. Proud to feel the pavement under me, reeling with feet. Feet tripping, skipping, lagging, dragging, plodding doggedly, or springing up and advancing on firm elastic insteps. A boy is selling papers, I smell them clean and new from the press. They are fresh like the air, and pungent as tulips and narcissus.

The blue sky pales to lemon, and great tongues of gold blind the shop-windows putting out their contents in a flood of flame.

Streets
(Adapted from the poet Yakura Sanjin, 1769)

As I wandered through the eight hundred and eight streets of
    the city,
I saw nothing so beautiful
As the Women of the Green Houses,
With their girdles of spun gold,
And their long-sleeved dresses,
Coloured like the graining of wood.

As they walk,
The hems of their outer garments flutter open,
And the blood-red linings glow like sharp-toothed maple
  leaves
In Autumn.

Yoshiwara Lament

Golden peacocks
Under blossoming cherry-trees,
But on all the wide sea
There is no boat.

Circumstance

Upon the maple leaves
The dew shines red,
But on the lotus blossom
It has the pale transparence of tears.

Autumn

All day I have watched the purple vine leaves
Fall into the water.
And now in the moonlight they still fall,
But each leaf is fringed with silver.

Illusion

Walking beside the tree-peonies
I saw a beetle
Whose wings were of black lacquer
    spotted with milk.
I would have caught it,
But it ran from me swiftly
And hid under the stone lotus
Which supports the statue of Buddha.

Autumn Haze

Is it a dragonfly or a maple leaf
That settles softly down upon the water?

Middle Age

Like black ice
Scrolled over with unintelligible patterns
    by an ignorant skater
Is the dulled surface of my heart.

MARIANNE MOORE

A Talisman

Under a splintered mast,
torn from the ship and cast
          near her hull,

a stumbling shepherd found
embedded in the ground,
          a sea-gull

of lapis lazuli,
a scarab of the sea,
          with wings spread –

curling its coral feet,
parting its beak to greet
          men long dead.

He Made This Screen

not of silver nor of cord,
but of weather-beaten laurel.

Here, he introduced a sea
uniform like tapestry;

here a fig-tree; there, a face;
there, a dragon circling space –

designating here, a bower;
there, a pointed passion-flower.

You Are Like the Realistic Product of an Idealistic Search for Gold at the Foot of the Rainbow

Hid by the august foliage and fruit
   of the grape vine,
   twine
     your anatomy
       round the pruned and polished stem,
             chameleon.
             Fire laid upon
         an emerald as long as
         the Dark King's massy
     one,
could not snap the spectrum up for food
   as you have done.

Δ'ΩΡΙΑ
(D.I.)

Be in me as the eternal moods
    of the bleak wind, and not
As transient things are –
    gaiety of flowers.
Have me in strong loneliness
    of sunless cliffs
And of grey waters.
    Let the gods speak softly of us
In days hereafter,
    The shadowy flowers of Orcus
Remember thee.

The Return

See, they return; ah, see the tentative
Movements, and the slow feet,
The trouble in the pace and the uncertain
Wavering!
See, they return, one, and by one,
With fear, as half-awakened;
As if the snow should hesitate
And murmur in the wind,
              and half turn back;
These were the "Wing'd-with-Awe",
              Inviolable.
Gods of the wingèd shoe!

With them the silver hounds,
                    sniffing the trace of air!
Haie! Haie!
          These were the swift to harry;
These the keen-scented;
These were the souls of blood.

Slow on the leash,
                    pallid the leash-men!

After Ch'u Yuan
(D.I.)

I will get me to the wood
Where the gods walk garlanded in wistaria,
By the silver-blue flood
    move others with ivory cars.
There come forth many maidens
    to gather grapes for the leopards, my friend,
For there are leopards drawing the cars.

I will walk in the glade,
I will come out from the new thicket
    and accost the procession of maidens.

Liu Ch'e
(D.I.)

The rustling of silk is discontinued,
Dust drifts over the courtyard,
There is no sound of footfall, and the leaves
Scurry into heaps and lie still,
And she the rejoicer of the heart is beneath them:

A wet leaf that clings to the threshold.

Fan-piece, for her Imperial Lord
(D.I.)

O fan of white silk,
    clear as frost on the grass-blade,
You also are laid aside.

Ts'ai Chi'h
(D.I.)

The petals fall in the fountain,
    the orange-coloured rose-leaves,
Their ochre clings to the stone.

In a Station of the Metro

The apparition of these faces in the crowd;
Petals on a wet, black bough.

The Garden

En robe de parade. SAMAIN

Like a skein of loose silk blown against a wall
She walks by the railing of a path
    in Kensington Gardens,
And she is dying piece-meal
    of a sort of emotional anaemia.

And around about there is a rabble
Of the filthy, sturdy, unkillable infants of the very poor.
They shall inherit the earth.

In her is the end of breeding.
Her boredom is exquisite and excessive.
She would like some one to speak to her,
And is almost afraid that I
        will commit that indiscretion.

Alba

As cool as the pale wet leaves
        of lily-of-the-valley
She lay beside me in the dawn.

Heather

The black panther treads at my side,
And above my fingers
There float the petal-like flames.

The milk-white girls
Unbend from the holly-trees,
And their snow-white leopard
Watches to follow our trace.

Albatre

This lady in the white bath-robe which she calls a peignoir,
Is, for the time being, the mistress of my friend,
And the delicate white feet of her little dog
Are not more delicate than she is,
Nor would Gautier himself have despised their contrasts in
    whiteness
As she sits in the great chair
Between the two indolent candles.

The Encounter

All the while they were talking the new morality
Her eyes explored me.
And when I arose to go
Her fingers were like the tissue
Of a Japanese paper napkin.

A Girl

The tree has entered my hands,
The sap has ascended my arms,
The tree has grown in my breast –
Downward,
The branches grow out of me, like arms.

Tree you are,
Moss you are,
You are violets with wind above them.
A child – *so* high – you are,
And all this is folly to the world.

ALLEN UPWARD

From *Scented Leaves from a Chinese Jar*
(D.I.)

THE MERMAID

The sailor boy who leant over the side of the Junk of Many Pearls, and combed the green tresses of the sea with his ivory fingers, believing that he had heard the voice of a mermaid, cast his body down between the waves.

THE MILKY WAY

My mother taught me that every night a procession of junks carrying lanterns moves silently across the sky, and the water sprinkled from their paddles falls to the earth in the form of dew. I no longer believe that the stars are junks carrying lanterns, no longer that the dew is shaken from their oars.

THE SEA-SHELL

To the passionate lover, whose sighs come back to him on every breeze, all the world is like a murmuring sea-shell.

WILLIAM CARLOS WILLIAMS

Postlude
(D.I.)

Now that I have cooled to you
Let there be gold of tarnished masonry,
Temples soothed by the sun to ruin
That sleep utterly.
Give me hand for the dances,
Ripples at Philae, in and out,
And lips, my Lesbian,
Wall flowers that once were flame.

Your hair is my Carthage
And my arms the bow,
And our words arrows
To shoot the stars
Who from the misty sea
Swarm to destroy us.
But you're there beside me –
Oh, how shall I defy you
Who wound me in the night
With breasts shining
Like Venus and like Mars?
The night that is shouting Jason
When the loud eaves rattle
As with waves above me
Blue at the prow of my desire!
O prayers in the dark!
O incense to Poseidon!
Calm in Atlantis.

Fire Spirit

I am old.
You warm yourselves at these fires?
In the center of these flames
I sit, my teeth chatter!
Where shall I turn for comfort?

To Mark Anthony in Heaven

This quiet morning light
reflected, how many times
from grass and trees and clouds
enters my north room
touching the walls with
grass and clouds and trees.
Anthony,
trees and grass and clouds.
Why did you follow
that beloved body
with your ships at Actium?
I hope it was because
you knew her inch by inch
from slanting feet upward
to the roots of her hair
and down again and that
you saw her
above the battle's fury –
clouds and trees and grass –

For then you are
listening in heaven.

Portrait of a Lady

Your thighs are appletrees
whose blossoms touch the sky.
Which sky? The sky
where Watteau hung a lady's
slipper. Your knees
are a southern breeze – or
a gust of snow. Agh! what
sort of man was Fragonard?
– as if that answered
anything. Ah, yes – below
the knees, since the tune
drops that way, it is
one of those white summer days,
the tall grass of your ankles
flickers upon the shore –
Which shore? –
the sand clings to my lips –
Which shore?
Agh! petals maybe. How
should I know?
Which shore? Which shore?
I said petals from an appletree.

The Shadow

Soft as the bed in the earth
where a stone has lain –
so soft, so smooth and so cool
Spring closes me in
with her arms and her hands.

Rich as the smell
of new earth on a stone
that has lain breathing
the damp through its pores –
Spring closes me in
with her blossomy hair
brings dark to my eyes.

Metric Figure

There is a bird in the poplars!
It is the sun!
The leaves are little yellow fish
swimming in the river.
The bird skims above them,
day is on his wings.
Phoebus!
It is he that is making
the great gleam among the poplars!
It is his singing
outshines the noise
of leaves clashing in the wind.

Summer Song

Wanderer moon
smiling a
faintly ironical smile
at this
brilliant, dew-moistened
summer morning, –
a detached
sleepily indifferent
smile, a
wanderer's smile, –
if I should
buy a shirt
your color and
put on a necktie
sky-blue
where would they carry me?

THE IMAGISTS AFTER IMAGISM

Poems that appeared
in the *Imagist Anthology 1930*
are noted: 1930

RICHARD ALDINGTON

From *Passages Toward a Long Poem*
(1930)

I

Troy's down
and an old woman nods in the sun,
Electra:

'She with her eyes, and hair
red as the blood on her slender hands,
and swift eddy of passions,
dust in the rock-tomb under the gold garments.

Kings shed blood for her sake –
and I, the virtuous, the serf's bride,
an old woman trembling in chilly sunlight,
a king's daughter,
but not the lover or mother of kings.

Great deeds were wrought by the King, my father,
but the passion in a woman's blood
swept him moaning to the grave.

No man has shed blood for my sake.

I armed my brother's hand
but shrank and trembled and wept
when the sword pierced her womb,
the woman men loved.

It was I who killed her;
who but a woman could have hated her so much?
Cold, cold, and an end to her hot loves.

But who has loved me,
what man shed blood for my sake?'

Troy's down,
long down
and an old woman trembles in the sun.

VII

They say the lion and
but here lizards life-flashes
over stormy rocks why
do the english hate life
but so does raucous italy
fingering cento lire
                but
that oleander mouth is
diverse spirit wavering
                   in agate eyes
the inner fire consumes
                  and life renews

If You Will Let Me Sing

If you will let me sing,
that God will be
gracious to each of us,
who found his own wild Daphne
in a tree,
who set
on desolate plinth,
image
of Hyacinth.

Epitaph

So I may say,
'I died of living,
having lived one hour';

so they may say,
'she died soliciting
illicit fervour';

so you may say,
'Greek flower; Greek ecstasy
reclaims for ever

one who died
following
intricate songs' lost measure.'

The Flowering Of The Rod
(extract)

I

O the beautiful garment,
the beautiful raiment –

do not think of His face
or even His hands,

do not think how we will stand
before Him;

remember the snow
on Hermon;

do not look below
where the blue gentian

reflects geometric pattern
in the ice-floe;

do not be beguiled
by the geometry of perfection

for even now,
the terrible banner

darkens the bridge-head;
we have shown

that we could stand;
we have withstood

the anger, frustration,
bitter fire of destruction;

leave the smouldering cities below
(we have done what we could),

we have given until we have no more to give;
alas, it was pity, rather than love, we gave;

now having given all, let us leave all;
above all, let us leave pity

and mount higher
to love – resurrection.

II

I go where I love and where I am loved,
into the snow;

I go to the things I love
with no thought of duty or pity;

I go where I belong, inexorably,
as the rain that has lain long

in the furrow; I have given
or would have given

life to the grain;
but if it will not grow or ripen

with the rain of beauty,
the rain will return to the cloud;

the harvester sharpens his steel on the stone;
but this is not our field.

we have not sown this;
pitiless, pitiless, let us leave

The-place-of-a-skull
to those who have fashioned it.

III

In resurrection, there is confession
if we start to argue; if we stand and stare,

we do not know where to go;
in resurrection, this is simple affirmation,

but do not delay to round up the others,
up and down the street; your going

in a moment like this, is the best proof
that you know the way;

does the first wild-goose stop to explain
to the others? no – he is off;

they follow or not,
that is their affair;

does the first wild-goose care
whether the others follow or not?

I do not think so – he is so happy to be off –
he knows where he is going;

so we must be drawn or we must fly,
like the snow-geese of the Arctic circle,

to the Carolinas or to Florida,
or like those migratory flocks

who still (they say) hover
over the lost island, Atlantis;

seeking what we once knew,
we know ultimately we will find

happiness; *today shalt thou be
with me in Paradise.*

IV

Blue-geese, white-geese, you may say,
yes, I know this duality, this double nostalgia!

I know the insatiable longing
in winter, for palm-shadow

and sand and burnt sea-drift;
but in the summer, as I watch

the wave till its edge of foam
touches the hot sand and instantly

vanishes like snow on the equator,
I would cry out, stay, stay;

then I remember the delicate enduring frost
and its mid-winter dawn-pattern;

in the hot noon-sun, I think of the grey
opalescent winter-dawn; as the wave

burns on the shingle, I think,
you are less beautiful than frost;

but it is also true that I pray,
O, give me burning blue

and brittle burnt sea-weed
above the tide-line,

as I stand, still unsatisfied,
under the long shadow-on-snow of the pine.

JOHN GOULD FLETCHER

Demolition of the Waldorf-Astoria
New York, May 1929
(1930)

I

Chocolate-brown walls with tablets clamped in jaws
Of lions: dark ring-bearing claws
Depending from great flag-poles that outspring
Over the pavement: what do these things bring?

Here morning, noon, and night
Behind archèd windows looped against the light
With silken curtains, hands have lifted knives
And forks against the tide of human lives.

Passing and forever passing, day on day,
Envious or indifferent to the array
Of tablets set with silver, glass, and flowers:
While out beyond the flag-poles marched the hours

Of festive days with their contending folds
Of broad striped banners. Now this moment rolls
A quarter century from my mind that sees
Them bellying outward stiffly in the breeze

That blows up half-a-mile of harness-reins,
And agitated bitts and hooves and manes.
Rattling forever onward towards a shore
That soon will never find them any more.

II

Through my lone listening creeps the sudden din
Of glittering picks that hack their way within
Green cupolaèd turrets and start slowly down;
A flash of blue sky through the chocolate brown

Of walls rent open. Downwards are out-rolled
Upon the pavement costly marbles, gold
Mosaic and deep leather armchairs where
Cigar-smoke once stole out in superheated air.

Long tapering fingers languidly lifting spoons,
Now, blunt and squat, lift shovels. Under the moons
Of table lamps, the looped and creamy weight
Of floating curtains split, lets loose the freight

Of orchids and bright napery pell-mell thrown
Into iron trucks along with crumbled brick and stone.

III

What can I gather, seize
From hungry pell-mell years;
What memories can I pile
Beside this shattered wall?

Roses that bloomed unsung
Beside a garden-path,
Great gold chrysanthemums
Like the sun's disk over slaty-blue mountains descending.

Wild violets, shy, remote;
Magnolias late remembered,
The folded sleep of poppies
Set in the seeded grass.

Asters that blazed when love
Entered at last my heart;
Purple mesquite that puffed
Its smoke-balls out into the thunderous morning;

Heaped peonies, rhododendrons
Like silken rajahs set on thrones of jade;
Valleys where bluebells hung,
A lonely lake under the still grey trees;

And these forget-me-nots
That once I saw beside a birch-fringed pond;
Reflecting into the waters their pure tint,
A colour more remote and still than any sky.

These are the memories that upon the screen
Of mind I brush, to mark eternal transience there;
The screen is folded up, and thrown away;
And in its stead I face the surge of death.

IV

A boy's face pressed against a darkening pane;
Without the city alters; slow the rain
Specks the grey pavements where the landaus rolled
Their waves of luxury through the sunset's gold;
Springtide of life comes now; he does not guess
How soon that pageant fades to nothingness.

And years come fast, and many years go past,
Love bitter-sweet smiles, beckoning, and at last
Love is a painful hope; wars come and earth
Is shaken, pallid, waiting a new birth;
Far from the glossy carriages, and the dreams
Of laden harvest-fields by bank-full streams.

Now streams of nickel and black-lacquered steel
Crawl slowly on, wheel against padded wheel,
And green and red and gold the lights burn out above
Clamorous streets; and few souls hope for love;
Patrician domes fall down, and leave the sky
Empty of meaning, travailing but to die.

D. H. LAWRENCE

Intimates
(1930)

Don't you care for my love? she said bitterly.

I handed her the mirror, and said:
Please address these questions to the proper person!
Please make all requests to headquarters!
In all matters of emotional importance
please approach the supreme authority direct! –
– So I handed her the mirror.

And she would have broken it over my head,
but she caught sight of her own reflection
and that held her spell-bound for two seconds
while I fled.

Ultimate Reality

A young man said to me:
I am interested in the problem of Reality.

I said: Really!
Then I saw him turn to glance, surreptitiously,
in the big mirror, at his own fascinating shadow.

Image-Making Love
(1930)

Always
at the core of me
burns a small flame of anger, gnawing
from trespassed contacts, from hot, digging-in fingers of love.

Always
in the eyes of those who loved me well
I have seen at last the image of him they loved
and took for me,
mistook for me.

And always
it was a pretty monkey that resembled me
and was a gibe at me.

So now I want, above all things
to preserve my nakedness
from the gibe and finger-clutch of image-making love.

Nothing to Save

There is nothing to save, now all is lost,
but a tiny core of stillness in the heart
like the eye of a violet.

Listen to the Band!

There is a band playing in the early night,
but it is only unhappy men making a noise
to drown their inner cacophony: and ours.

A little moon, quite still, leans and sings to herself
through the night
and the music of men is like a mouse gnawing,
gnawing in a wooden trap, trapped in.

AMY LOWELL

Wind and Silver

Greatly shining,
The Autumn moon floats in the thin sky;
And the fish-ponds shake their backs and
    flash their dragon scales
As she passes over them.

Fugitive

Sunlight,
Three marigolds,
And a dusky purple poppy-pod –
Out of these I made a beautiful world,
Will you have them –
Brightness,
Gold,
And a sleep with dreams?
They are brittle pleasures certainly,
But where can you find better?
Roses are not noted for endurance
And only thirty days are June.

If I Were Francesco Guardi

I

I think you are a white clematis
Climbing the wall of a seaside garden,
When there is a green haze on the water
And a boy is eating a melon in a boat
　with a brown sail.

II

I think you are the silver heart of a great square,
Holding little people like glass beads,
Watching them parade – parade – and gather,
When the sun slips to an opposite angle,
And a thunder of church bells lies like a bronze
　roof beneath the sky.

Autumn

A stand of people
by an open

grave underneath
the heavy leaves

celebrates
the cut and fill

for the new road
where

an old man
on his knees

reaps a basket-
ful of

matted grasses for
his goats

Rain
(1930)

As the rain moistens
everything
as does
        your love
bathe every
        open
object of the world –

In houses
the priceless dry
        rooms
of illicit love
where we live
hear the wash of the
         rain –

There
      paintings
and fine
      metalware
oven stuffs –
all the whoreishness
of our
      delight
sees
from its window
the spring wash
of your love
         the falling
rain –

the trees
are become
beasts fresh risen
from
      the sea –
      water

trickles
from the crevices of
their hides –

So my life is spent
  to keep out love
with which
she rains upon

123

the world
of spring
drips
so spreads
the words
far apart to let in
her love
and running in between
the drops
the rain
is a kind physician
the rain
of her thoughts over
the ocean
every

where

walking with
invisible swift feet
over

the helpless
waves –

Unworldly love
that has no hope
of the world

and that
cannot change the world
to its delight

the rain

falls upon the earth
and grass and flowers
come

perfectly
into form from its
liquid
clearness

But love is
unworldly
and nothing
comes of it but love
following
and falling endlessly
from
her thoughts –

APPENDICES

A.

FROM *POETRY* MARCH 1913

Imagisme*

Some curiosity has been aroused concerning *Imagisme*, and as I was unable to find anything definite about it in print, I sought out an *imagiste*, with intent to discover whether the group itself knew anything about the "movement." I gleaned these facts.

The *imagistes* admitted that they were contemporaries of the Post Impressionists and the Futurists; but they had nothing in common with these schools. They had not published a manifesto. They were not a revolutionary school; their only endeavor was to write in accordance with the best tradition, as they found it in the best writers of all time, – in Sappho, Catullus, Villon. They seemed to be absolutely intolerant of all poetry that was not written in such endeavor, ignorance of the best tradition forming no excuse. They had a few rules, drawn up for their own satisfaction only, and they had not published them. They were:

1. Direct treatment of the "thing," whether subjective or objective.
2. To use absolutely no word that did not contribute to the presentation.
3. As regarding rhythm: to compose in sequence of the musical phrase, not in sequence of a metronome.

By these standards they judged all poetry, and found most of it wanting. They held also a certain "Doctrine of the Image," which they had not committed to writing; they said that it did not concern the public, and would provoke useless discussion.

*Editor's Note – In response to many requests for information regarding *Imagism* and the *Imagistes*, we publish this note by Mr. Flint, supplementing it with further exemplification by Mr. Pound. It will be seen from these that *Imagism* is not necessarily associated with Hellenic subjects, or with *vers libre* as a prescribed form.

The devices whereby they persuaded approaching poetasters to attend their instruction were:

1. They showed him his own thought already splendidly expressed in some classic (and the school musters altogether a most formidable erudition).

2. They re-wrote his verses before his eyes, using about ten words to his fifty.

Even their opponents admit of them – ruefully – "At least they do keep bad poets from writing!"

I found among them an earnestness that is amazing to one accustomed to the usual London air of poetic dilettantism. They consider that Art is all science, all religon, philosophy and metaphysic. It is true that *snobisme* may be urged against them; but it is at least *snobisme* in its most dynamic form, with a great deal of sound sense and energy behind it; and they are stricter with themselves than with any outsider.

F. S. Flint

B.

A Few Don'ts By An Imagiste

An "Image" is that which presents an intellectual and emotional complex in an instant of time. I use the term "complex" rather in the technical sense employed by the newer psychologists, such as Hart, though we might not agree absolutely in our application.

It is the presentation of such a "complex" instantaneously which gives that sense of sudden liberation; that sense of freedom from time limits and space limits; that sense of sudden growth, which we experience in the presence of the greatest works of art.

It is better to present one Image in a lifetime than to produce voluminous works.

All this, however, some may consider open to debate. The immediate necessity is to tabulate A LIST OF DON'TS for those beginning to write verses. But I can not put all of them into Mosaic negative.

To begin with, consider the three rules recorded by Mr. Flint, not as dogma – never consider anything as dogma – but as the result of long contemplation, which, even if it is some one else's contemplation may be worth consideration.

Pay no attention to the criticism of men who have never themselves written a notable work. Consider the discrepancies between the actual writing of the Greek poets and dramatists, and the theories of the Graeco-Roman grammarians, concocted to explain their metres.

Language

Use no superfluous word, no adjective, which does not reveal something.

Don't use such an expression as "dim land *of peace.*" It dulls the image. It mixes an abstraction with the concrete. It comes from the writer's not realizing that the natural object is always the *adequate* symbol.

Go in fear of abstractions. Don't retell in mediocre verse what has already been done in good prose. Don't think any intelligent person is going to be deceived when you try to shirk all the difficulties of the unspeakably difficult art of good prose by chopping your composition into line lengths.

What the expert is tired of today the public will be tired of tomorrow.

Don't imagine that the art of poetry is any simpler than the art of music, or that you can please the expert before you have spent at least as much effort on the art of verse as the average piano teacher spends on the art of music.

Be influenced by as many great artists as you can, but have the decency either to acknowledge the debt outright, or to try to conceal it.

Don't allow "influence" to mean merely that you mop up the particular decorative vocabulary of some one or two poets whom you happen to admire. A Turkish war correspondent was recently caught red-handed babbling in his despatches of "dove-grey" hills, or else it was "pearl-pale", I can not remember.

Use either no ornament or good ornament.

Rhythm and Rhyme

Let the candidate fill his mind with the finest cadences he can discover, preferably in a foreign language,* so that the meaning of the words may be less likely to divert his attention from the movement; e.g. Saxon charms, Hebridean Folk Songs, the verse of Dante, and the lyrics of Shakespeare – if he can dissociate the vocabulary from the cadence. Let him dissect the lyrics of Goethe coldly into their component sound values, syllables long and short, stressed and unstressed, into vowels and consonants.

It is not necessary that a poem should rely on its music, but if it does rely on its music that music must be such as will delight the expert.

Let the neophyte know assonance and alliteration, rhyme immediate and delayed, simple and polyphonic, as a musician would expect to know harmony and counterpoint and all the minutiae of his craft. No time is too great to give to these matters or to any one of them, even if the artist seldom have need of them.

Don't imagine that a thing will "go" in verse just because it's too dull to go in prose.

Don't be "viewy" – leave that to the writers of pretty little philosophic essays. Don't be descriptive; remember that the painter can describe a landscape much better than you can, and that he has to know a deal more about it.

When Shakespeare talks of the 'Dawn in russet mantle clad' he presents something which the painter does not present. There is in this line of his nothing that one can call description; he presents.

Consider the way of the scientists rather than the way of an advertising agent for a new soap.

The scientist does not expect to be acclaimed as a great scientist until he has *discovered* something. He begins by learning what has been discovered already. He goes from that point onward. He does not bank on being a charming fellow personally. He does not expect his friends to applaud the results of his freshman class work. Freshmen in poetry are unfortunately not confined to a definite and recognizable

*This is for rhythm, his vocabulary must of course be found in his native tongue.

class room. They are "all over the shop". Is it any wonder "the public is indifferent to poetry?"

Don't chop your stuff into separate *iambs*. Don't make each line stop dead at the end, and then begin every next line with a heave. Let the beginning of the next line catch the rise of the rhythm wave, unless you want a definite longish pause.

In short, behave as a musician, a good musician, when dealing with that phase of your art which has exact parallels in music. The same laws govern, and you are bound by no others.

Naturally, your rhythmic structure should not destroy the shape of your words, or their natural sound, or their meaning. It is improbable that, at the start, you will be able to get a rhythm-structure strong enough to affect them very much, though you may fall a victim to all sorts of false stopping due to line ends and caesurae.

The Musician can rely on pitch and the volume of the orchestra. You can not. The term harmony is misapplied in poetry; it refers to simultaneous sounds of different pitch. There is, however, in the best verse a sort of residue of sound which remains in the ear of the hearer and acts more or less as an organ-base.

A rhyme must have in it some slight element of surprise if it is to give pleasure; it need not be bizarre or curious, but it must be well used if used at all.

Vide further Vildrac and Duhamel's notes on rhyme in '*Technique Poétique*'.

That part of your poetry which strikes upon the imaginative *eye* of the reader will lose nothing by translation into a foreign tongue; that which appeals to the ear can reach only those who take it in the original.

Consider the definiteness of Dante's presentation, as compared with Milton's rhetoric. Read as much of Wordsworth as does not seem too unutterably dull.

If you want the gist of the matter go to Sappho, Catullus, Villon, Heine when he is in the vein, Gautier when he is not too frigid; or, if you have not the tongues, seek out the leisurely Chaucer. Good prose will do you no harm, and there is good discipline to be had by trying to write it.

Translation is likewise good training, if you find that your original matter "wobbles" when you try to rewrite it. The meaning of the poem to be translated can not "wobble".

If you are using a symmetrical form, don't put in what you want to say and then fill up the remaining vacuums with slush.

Don't mess up the perception of one sense by trying to define it in terms of another. This is usually only the result of being too lazy to find the exact word. To this clause there are possibly exceptions.

The first three simple prescriptions will throw out nine-tenths of all the bad poetry now accepted as standard and classic; and will prevent you from many a crime of production.

'. . . *Mais d'abord il faut être un poète*', as MM. Duhamel and Vildrac have said at the end of their little book, '*Notes sur la Technique Poétique*'. *Ezra Pound*

C.

PREFACE TO *Some Imagist Poets 1915*

In March, 1914, a volume appeared entitled 'Des Imagistes'. It was a collection of the work of various young poets, presented together as a school. This school has been widely discussed by those interested in new movements in the arts, and has already become a household word. Differences of taste and judgment, however, have arisen among the contributors to that book; growing tendencies are forcing them along different paths. Those of us whose work appears in this volume have therefore decided to publish our collection under a new title, and we have been joined by two or three poets who did not contribute to the first volume, our wider scope making this possible.

In this new book we have followed a slightly different arrangement to that of the former Anthology. Instead of an arbitrary selection by an editor, each poet has been permitted to represent himself by the work he considers his best, the only stipulation being that it should not yet have appeared in book form. A sort of informal committee – consisting of more than half the authors here represented – have arranged the book and decided what should be printed and what omitted, but, as a general rule, the poets have been allowed absolute freedom in this direction, limitations of space only being imposed upon them.

Also, to avoid any appearance of precedence, they have been put in alphabetical order.

As it has been suggested that much of the misunderstanding of the former volume was due to the fact that we did not explain ourselves in a preface, we have thought it wise to tell the public what our aims are, and why we are banded together between one set of covers.

The poets in this volume do not represent a clique. Several of them are personally unknown to the others, but they are united by certain common principles, arrived at independently. These principles are not new; they have fallen into desuetude. They are the essentials of all great poetry, indeed of all great literature, and they are simply these:

1. To use the language of common speech, but to employ always the *exact* word, not the nearly-exact, nor the merely decorative word.

2. To create new rhythms – as the expression of new moods – and not to copy old rhythms, which merely echo old moods. We do not insist upon 'free-verse' as the only method of writing poetry. We fight for it as for a principle of liberty. We believe that the individuality of a poet may often be better expressed in free-verse than in conventional forms. In poetry, a new cadence means a new idea.

3. To allow absolute freedom in the choice of subject. It is not good art to write badly about aeroplanes and automobiles; nor is it necessarily bad art to write well about the past. We believe passionately in the artistic value of modern life, but we wish to point out that there is nothing so uninspiring nor so old-fashioned as an aeroplane of the year 1911.

4. To present an image (hence the name: "Imagist"). We are not a school of painters, but we believe that poetry should render particulars exactly and not deal in vague generalities, however magnificent and sonorous. It is for this reason that we oppose the cosmic poet, who seems to us to shirk the real difficulties of his art.

5. To produce poetry that is hard and clear, never blurred nor indefinite.

6. Finally, most of us believe that concentration is of the very essence of poetry.

The subject of free-verse is too complicated to be discussed here. We may say briefly, that we attach the term to all that increasing amount of writing whose cadence is more marked, more definite, and closer knit than that of prose, but which is not so violently nor so obviously accented as the so-called "regular verse." We refer those interested in the question to the Greek Melic poets, and to the many excellent French studies on the subject by such distinguished and well-equipped authors as Remy de Gourmont, Gustave Kahn, Georges Duhamel, Charles Vildrac, Henri Ghéon, Robert de Souza, André Spire, etc.

We wish it to be clearly understood that we do not represent an exclusive artistic sect; we publish our work together because of mutual artistic sympathy, and we propose to bring out our co-operative volume each year for a short term of years, until we have made a place for ourselves and our principles such as we desire.

PREFACE TO *Some Imagist Poets 1916*

In bringing the second volume of *Some Imagist Poets* before the public, the authors wish to express their gratitude for the interest which the 1915 volume aroused. The discussion of it was widespread, and even those critics out of sympathy with Imagist tenets accorded it much space. In the Preface to that book, we endeavoured to present those tenets in a succinct form. But the very brevity we employed has lead to a great deal of misunderstanding. We have decided, therefore, to explain the laws which govern us a little more fully. A few people may understand, and the rest can merely misunderstand again, a result to which we are quite accustomed.

In the first place "Imagism" does not mean merely the presentation of pictures. "Imagism" refers to the manner of presentation, not to the subject. It means a clear presentation of whatever the author wishes to convey. Now he may wish to convey a mood of indecision, in which case the poem should be indecisive; he may wish to bring before his reader the constantly shifting and changing lights over a landscape, or the varying attitudes of mind of a person under strong emotion, then his poem must shift and change to present this clearly. The "exact" word does not mean the word which exactly describes the object in itself, it means the "exact" word which brings the effect of that object before the reader as it presented itself to the poet's mind at the time of writing the poem. Imagists deal but little with similes, although much of their poetry is metaphorical. The reason for this is that while acknowledging the figure to be an integral part of all poetry, they feel that the constant imposing of one figure upon another in the same poem blurs the central effect.

The great French critic, Remy de Gourmont, wrote last Summer in *La France* that the Imagists were the descendants of the French *Symbolistes*. In the Preface to his *Livre des Masques*, M. de Gourmont has thus described *Symbolisme*: "Individualism in literature, liberty of art, abandonment of existing forms ... The sole excuse which a man can have for writing is to write down himself, to unveil for others the sort of world which mirrors itself in his individual glass ... He should create his own aesthetics – and we should admit as many aesthetics as there are original minds, and judge them for what they are and not what they are not." In this sense the Imagists are descendants of the *Symbolistes*; they are Individualists.

The only reason that Imagism has seemed so anarchaic and strange to English and American reviewers is that their minds do not easily and quickly suggest the steps by which modern art has arrived at its present position. Its immediate prototype cannot be found in English or American literature, we must turn to Europe for it. With Debussy and Stravinsky in music, and Gauguin and Matisse in painting, it should have been evident to every one that art was entering upon an era of change. But music and painting are universal languages, so we have become accustomed to new idioms in them, while we still find it hard to recognize a changed idiom in literature.

The crux of the situation is just here. It is in the idiom employed. Imagism asks to be judged by different standards from those employed in Nineteenth-Century art. It is small wonder that Imagist poetry should be incomprehensible to men whose sole touchstone for art is the literature of one country for a period of four centuries. And it is an illuminating fact that among poets and men conversant with many poetic idioms, Imagism is rarely misconceived. They may not agree with us, but they do not misunderstand us.

This must not be misconstrued into the desire to belittle our forerunners. On the contrary, the Imagists have the greatest admiration for the past, and humility towards it. But they have been caught in the throes of a new birth. The exterior world is changing, and with it men's feelings, and every age must express its feelings in its own individual way. No art is any more 'egoistic' than another; all art is an attempt to express the feelings of the artist, whether it be couched in narrative form or employ a more personal expression.

It is not what Imagists write about which makes them hard of comprehension; it is the way they write it. All nations have laws of prosody, which undergo changes from time to time. The laws of English metrical prosody are well known to every one concerned with the subject. But that is only one form of prosody. Other nations have had different ones: Anglo-Saxon poetry was founded upon alliteration, Greek and Roman was built upon quantity, the Oriental was formed out of repetition, and the Japanese Hokku got its effects by an exact and never-to-be-added-to series of single syllables. So it is evident that poetry can be written in many modes. That the Imagists base much of their poetry upon cadence and not upon metre makes them neither good nor bad. And no one realizes more than they that no theories nor rules make poetry. They claim for their work only that it is sincere.

It is this very fact of "cadence" which has misled so many reviewers, until some have been betrayed into saying that the Imagists discard rhythm, when rhythm is the most important quality in their technique. The definition of *vers libre* is – a verse-form based upon cadence. Now cadence in music is one thing, cadence in poetry quite another, since we are not dealing with tone but with rhythm. It is the sense of perfect balance of flow and rhythm. Not only must the syllables so fall as to increase and continue the movement, but the whole poem must be as rounded and recurring as the circular swing of a balanced pendulum. It can be fast or slow, it may even jerk, but this perfect swing it must have, even its jerks must follow the central movement. To illustrate: Suppose a person were given the task of walking, or running, round a large circle, with two minutes given to do it in. Two minutes which he would just consume if he walked round the circle quietly. But in order to make the task easier for him, or harder, as the case might be, he was required to complete each half of the circle in exactly a minute. No other restrictions were placed upon him. He might dawdle in the beginning, and run madly to reach the half-circle mark on time, and then complete his task by walking steadily round the second half to goal. Or he might leap, and run, and skip, and linger in all sorts of ways, making up for slow going by fast, and for extra haste by pauses, and varying these movements on either lap of the circle as the humour seized him, only so that he were just one minute in traversing the first half-circle, and just one minute in traversing the second. Another illustration which may be employed is that of a Japanese wood-carving where a toad in one corner is balanced by a spray of blown flowers in the opposite upper one. The flowers are not the same shape as the toad, neither are they the same size, but the balance is preserved.

The unit in *vers libre* is not the foot, the number of the syllables, the quantity, or the line. The unit is the strophe, which may be the whole poem, or may be only a part. Each strophe is a complete circle: in fact, the meaning of the Greek word 'strophe' is simply that part of the poem which was recited while the chorus were making a turn round the altar set up in the centre of the theatre. The simile of the circle is more than a simile, therefore; it is a fact. Of course the circle need not always be the same size, nor need the times allowed to negotiate it be always the same. There is room here for an infinite number of variations. Also, circles can be added to circles, movement upon movement, to the poem, provided each movement completes itself, and ramifies naturally into the next. But one thing must be borne in mind: a cadenced poem is written to be read aloud, in this way only will its rhythm be felt. Poetry is a spoken and not a written art.

The *vers libristes* are often accused of declaring that they have discovered a new thing. Where such an idea started, it is impossible to say, certainly none of the better *vers libristes* was ever guilty of so ridiculous a statement. The name *vers libre* is new, the thing, most emphatically, is not. Not new in English poetry, at any rate. You will find something very much like it in Dryden's *Threnodia Augustalis*; a great deal of Milton's *Samson Agonistes* is written in it; and Matthew Arnold's *Philomela* is a shining example of it. Practically all of Henley's *London Voluntaries* are written in it, and (so potent are names) until it was christened *vers libre*, no one thought of objecting to it. But the oldest reference to *vers libre* is to be found in Chaucer's *House of Fame*, where the Eagle addresses the Poet in these words:

> And nevertheless hast set thy wyt
> Although that in thy heed full lyte is
> To make bookes, songes, or dytees
> In rhyme or elles in cadence.

Commentators have wasted reams of paper in an endeavour to determine what Chaucer meant by this. But is it not possible that he meant a verse based upon rhythm, but which did not follow the strict metrical prosody of his usual practice?

One of the charges frequently brought against the Imagists is that they write, not poetry, but "shredded prose". This misconception springs from the almost complete ignorance of the public in regard to the laws of cadenced verse. But, in fact, what is prose and what is poetry? Is it merely a matter of typographical arrangement? Must everything which is printed in equal lines, with rhymes at the ends, be called poetry, and everything which is printed in a block be called prose? Aristotle, who certainly knew more about this subject than any one else, declares in his *Rhetoric* that prose is rhythmical without being metrical (that is to say, without insistence on any single rhythm), and then goes on to state the feet that are employed in prose, making, incidentally, the remark that the iambic prevailed in ordinary conversation. The fact is, that there is no hard and fast dividing line between prose and poetry. As a French poet of distinction, Paul Fort, has said: "Prose and poetry are but one instrument, graduated." It is not a question of typography; it is not even a question of rules and forms. Poetry is the vision in a man's soul which he translates as best he can with the means at his disposal.

We are young, we are experimentalists, but we ask to be judged by our own standards, not by those which have governed other men at other times.

D.
LETTER FROM EZRA POUND TO
HARRIET MONROE

Coleman's Hatch, January 1915

Dear H.M.: ———— Poetry must be *as well written as prose*. Its language must be a fine language, departing in no way from speech save by a heightened intensity (i.e. simplicity). There must be no book words, no periphrases, no inversions. It must be as simple as De Maupassant's best prose, and as hard as Stendhal's.

There must be no interjections. No words flying off to nothing. Granted one can't get perfection every shot, this must be one's INTENTION.

Rhythm MUST have meaning. It can't be merely a careless dash off, with no grip and no real hold to the words and sense, a tumty tum tumty tum tum ta.

There must be no clichés, set phrases, stereotyped journalese. The only escape from such is by precision, a result of concentrated attention to what one is writing. The test of a writer is his ability for such concentration AND for his power to stay concentrated till he gets to the end of his poem, whether it is two lines or two hundred.

Objectivity and again objectivity, and expression: no hindside-beforeness, no straddled adjectives (as 'addled mosses dank'), no Tennysonianness of speech; nothing – nothing that you couldn't, in some circumstance, in the stress of some emotion, actually say. Every literaryism, every book word, fritters away a scrap of the reader's patience, a scrap of his sense of your sincerity. When one really feels and thinks, one stammers with simple speech; it is only in the flurry, the shallow frothy excitement of writing, or the inebriety of a metre, that one falls into the easy – oh, how easy! – speech of books and poems that one has read.*

* 1937. It should be realized that Ford Madox Ford had been hammering this point of view into me from the time I first met him (1908 or 1909) and that I owe him anything that I don't owe myself for having saved me from the academic influences then raging in London. –*E.P. January* 1937. (Footnote from Harriet Monroe's *A Poet's Life*.)

Language is made out of concrete things. General expressions in non-concrete terms are a laziness; they are talk, not art, not creation. They are the reaction of things on the writer, not a creative act *by* the writer.

'Epithets' are usually abstractions – I mean what they call 'epithets' in the books about poetry. The only adjective that is worth using is the adjective that is essential to the sense of the passage, not the decorative frill adjective.

Aldington has his occasional concentrations, and for that reason it is always possible that he will do a fine thing. There is a superficial cleverness in him, then a great and lamentable gap, then the hard point, the true centre, out of which a fine thing may come at any time.

Fletcher is sputter, bright flash, sputter. Impressionist temperament, made intense at half-seconds.

H.D. and William C. Williams both better emotional equipment than Aldington, but lacking the superficial cleverness. Ought to produce really fine things at great intervals.

Eliot is intelligent, very, but I don't know him well enough to make predictions.

Masters hits rock bottom now and again. He should comb the journalese out of his poems. I wish Lindsay all possible luck but we're not really pulling the same way, though we both pull against entrenched senility. — — — —

Sandburg may come out all right, but he needs to learn a *lot* about *How to Write*. I believe his intention is right.

Would to God I could see a bit more Sophoclean severity in the ambitions of mes amis et confrères. The general weakness of the writers of the new school is looseness, lack of rhythmical construction and intensity; secondly, an attempt to 'apply decoration', to use what ought to be a vortex as a sort of bill-poster, or fence-wash. Hinc illae lachrymae. Too bad about Amy – why can't she conceive of herself as a Renaissance figure instead of a spiritual chief, which she ain't.

Ebbene – enough of this.

LETTER FROM F. S. FLINT TO J. C. SQUIRE

65 Highbury New Park, N

29th January 1917

Dear Squire,

I am glad to have yr letter in reply to my rambling rumble-grumble, and, if I take up the debate, you wont curse me for a bore, I hope. First of all, you say that the reason why the papers will not print Imagist poems (we haven't given them much chance, by the way; the American reviews are much more lucrative) is because they do not like them. To that I reply that the English papers, with few exceptions, do not know, are not in a position to know or to say, what they like or dislike. English papers are provincial and in the true sense of the word illiterate. They understand nothing that comes to them first hand, and they accept work only when it has been vouched for for them by France, or Germany, or Italy, or Ireland. There is in the English papers no real conception of literature, no liberty of thought, and no ideas. Conceptions and forms that are of common acceptance in Paris or Berlin or Petrograd are looked at askance here, and, if an English poet dares to use them, he is treated with ignorant contempt. Read Mr Bourdillon on the Imagistes in the Times of two weeks back; there you have England. I think, by the way, that your remark that the writer of the article on the Imagists in the Times was in "a blue funk lest he should prove to have undervalued what posterity might think good" is rather gratuitous. I dont know who the man is myself; and I could not make your inference from the only evidence of the article. However, even if the *Times* is determined to keep abreast of the times, as you say, is not that an honourable fault? Is it not the real purpose of every journal, and are the Nation and (permit me!) the New Statesman to be praised for being "advanced", in their front pages and (permit me again!) reactionary in their rear pages. This is a curious phenomenon that our most liberal papers politically are our most reactionary papers in literature (among those that count, that is – I dont count the *Saturday Review* or the *Spectator*, for instance – and I add to these the *New Age*, for which, by the by, you and I have both been the verse critic, O ironie!). Suppose I suggest, in the interests of English literature, that the political and literary writers in the three papers I have named change places. I'm sure that politics would benefit, at least!

And now will you let me show you that you have given away the whole of your case against Imagism. (By the way, I hope you are taking all this in good part, *as it leaves me at present*!). You say, ''But a certain regularity of rhythm is the distinguishing mark of verse''. *Je te crois, César*! But we dont want to write verse, we dont profess to write verse, we wouldnt care if not another verse was written *d'ici aux Kalendes grecques*. We want to abolish verse, which, as Professor Mackail* said in his long review of our Latin and Greek translations, a review which appeared in the Times and was mainly devoted to H.D.'s choruses from Euripides, ''*is all in English a naturalised exotic*'',† and he praised our *return* to the true English tradition. Now then, sir, if we do not want verse, we certainly want poetry, and, if we give you *poetry*, what more do you ask, and why do you not print it, or rather, I should say, in fairness to you, since we have not sent much if any of our work, why do you object to it? You reply, ''One does at least ask that the rhythms fluctuate in accordance with the feeling and the thought''. So do we, precisely. You have not read the best of Aldington, H.D. and Fletcher, if you have not seen that this best fulfils the conditions. One does not want stuff that is ''merely shapeless and soundless''. One does not, indeed; but I do not agree with you that the words you quote are either (I believe they are from Aldington, but the book is in another room, and I'll verify it later on). You can print them.‡

*Flint's footnote: "He did not sign; but we know it was Mackail."

†The whole quotation is underlined, ''all'' and ''naturalised exotic'' have extra underlinings.

‡Flint wrote in the margin here: 'I thought this was from one of Aldington's poems 'From the scullery window' or some such title; but I can't lay my hand on the poem. You may have made it up; the argument is unaffected, however, if so.' Flint may have had A.'s poem 'Evening' in mind (*Images*, 1910–15), which ends 'And here am I looking wantonly at her/Over the kitchen sink.'

> I watch
> From the high window,
> And behind the dark
> Tossing poplars
> A blood-red moon
> Gyrates and leers,
> O Selene!

Or as:

I watch from the high window, and, behind the dark, tossing poplars, a blood-red moon gyrates and leers, O Selene!

And there is still good sound in them and good shape. If they ran in a rhyme scheme like this, abbacbc, you would probably not object to them. But the main point about them is, Do they with their context embody an emotion which in its expression makes a poem? Whether they are prose or verse is besdie [*sic*] the question; whether they are printed in regular or irregular lines is of no consequence, except that, printed irregularly, they are easier to read, and the rhythmic intention is better marked. But prose? *Il n'y a pas de prose, si ce n'est à la quatrième page des journaux.* Prose and verse, prose and verse: the rocks on which all English criticism of peotry [*sic*] breaks. What do you call the form of Gide, in *Le Roi Candaule*, of Claudel, in all his odes dramas [*sic*], of Vildrac, in *le Livre d'Amour*, of Fort, in his *Ballades Francaises*, of Peguy, in his *Mystères*, of Porché in *le Dessous du Masque*? Prose or verse, and, if not verse, therefore not poetry? Come, come!

Of course, we have never, as Imagists, claimed to have invented the moon. We do not pretend that our ideas are original. All that we wish to do is to place gently in evidence certain principles of the art of writing which journalism has submerged. We do not wish to claim your regard because of our novelty. Vers libre was written by Euripides, in spite of the professors. We wish to be considered as poets, first of all, and our writings to be judged by the poetic emotion and vision in them. We do say, of course, in justification of our form, that much poetic emotion is strangled and lost in the attempt to thrust it into the strait jacket* of regular metre and rhyme, that there is no

*Flint's footnote: "Much so-called poetry is merely a more or less clever and successful fitting of this jacket, i.e. the jacket often makes the poem."

intrinsic merit in metre, and that rhyme is a childish sort of trick; that a poetic emotion and vision is better expressed by letting the words come freely, controlled only by whatever art of writing and sense of style you may possess. If we are trivial or incoherent in anything we write, then we have written a bad poem that is all. Of course, we write bad poems; but, on the other hand, some of us have written some damn good poems too. Read H.D.'s *Sea Garden*. If you find triviality there ...! Read Fletcher's *Old House*. Read Aldington [*sic*] *Myrrhine & Konollis*. And dont condemn our good work because we have done bad.

I dare say you are pretty bored with all this by now. Let me console you by telling you that, interrupted, I have forgotten a great deal of what I set out to say. I wanted to talk a little more at length on the *ignorance*, the very real ignorance, that is almost the distinguishing mark of English criticism. The man who reviewed my translation of Verhaeren's *Love Poems* in the Nation talked of Maeterlinck, Verhaeren and *M. Cammaerts* (like that!) as representing Belgian literature, and this in an incoherent opening paragraph of a review in which he crabbed me. The same man (the style is the same) talks of Gibson's *blank verse* in a passage that is heavily rhymed. But this is an ignorance of lack of knowledge which a schoolmaster might have. Of the fundamental principles of literature, of the art of writing ... gawd!

Pour terminer, I like this little imagist poem:

> And evening falls,
> fusing tree and water and stone
> into a violet cloth,
> and the frail ash-tree hisses with a soft sharpness,
> like a fall of mounded grain;
> and a steamer, softly puffing along the river,
> passes, drawing a file of barges:
> and silence falls again.
> A bell tones; and the evening darkens;
> and sparsely along the other bank
> the greenish lights well out.*

*Flint's footnote: "With one or two stylist [*sic*] changes, which improve the style moreover, I have turned Squire's poem into what he calls prose." The last

Your critics, accustomed to look upon you as a very clever fellow, are rather puzzled when you give them a poem to bite at. It amuses me, this.

Yours sincerely,
F. S. Flint.

P.S.–Dont regard this as a considered statement. It is more or less what I mean, or, rather, it more or less expresses some of the obvious parts of my thoughts on this subject.

---

two lines are altered in Flint's hand to read: "and sparsely the greenish lights well out along the other bank."

'[This poem] was written one evening at a literary party in London, when H.D. and Flint, finding themselves sitting in a corner, both rather shy and "out of it", challenged each other to write a sonnet. H.D. did not complete hers, but Flint's was as follows . . .'

Glenn Hughes: *Imagism and the Imagists*

From *Otherworld*: *Cadences* by F. S. Flint

To a Young Lady
Who Moved Shyly Among Men
of Reputed Worth

The olive sky shone through the birch's lace
Of hanging leaves. The silken air was still.
London was beautiful. A tender thrill
Of sunset shook throughout the evening's grace.

Under an apple tree I stood a space,
And watched the birds hop on the lawn, until
Darkness had bent all image to his will,
When, oh! upon the rapt sky dawned your face!

Be brave, O Moon, lonely among the stars.
Be unrebuked and radiant, they will pale;
And Earth will love you for your loveliness.

My brain beats madly at the golden bars
That stay it, and my heart would have me scale
The moonlit branches where the night winds press.

(For the Imagist version of the same poem see p. 75 – 'London'.)

From *In The Net Of The Stars* by F. S. Flint

A Swan Song

Among the lily leaves the swan,
The pale, cold lily leaves, the swan,
With mirrored neck, a silver streak,
Tipped with a tarnished copper beak,
Toward the dark arch floats slowly on;
The water is deep and black beneath the arches.
The fishes quiver in the pool
Under the lily shadow cool,
And ripples gilded by the whin,
Painted, too, with a gloom of green,
Mingled with lilac blue and mauve,
Dropped from an overhanging grove;
White rose of flame the swan beneath the arches.

And, Earth! my heart if weary this hot noon
Of bearing life, your strange and secret gift.
Lying upon this bank, I hear the rune
Of springtime music, with my soul adrift
Upon its stagnant waters, wondering why
Thus rudderless I float askirt a shore,
A drear savannah, Death.
                    With ardent eye,
Inflamed with dreams of death and ancient lore,
The wild swan watched and waited for the end
Two hundred years of life its white wings bore.
And I in weary truth my song would blend, –
O heart of sombre lilies, why not now? –
A broken music, with the swan's full tone; –
For are you not alone? – ......
(plus 41 more lines)

(For the Imagist version of this poem see page 80 'The Swan')

F.
FROM NEW YORK *SUN*
9 MAY 1915

Ballade of Worshippers of the Image
by Conrad Aiken

Ezra Pound, Dick Aldington,
  Fletcher and Flint and sweet H.D.,
Whether you chirp in Kensington
  Or Hampstead Heath, or Bloomsbury;
Birds of protean pedigree,
  Vorticist, Cubist, or Imagist,
Where in a score of years will you be,
  And the delicate succubae you kissed?

You, of the trivial straining fun,
  Who ape your betters in mirthless glee;
You, whose meticulous clear lines run
  In hideous insipidity;
And you, forsooth, who shinned a tree
  To keep with the gaping moon your tryst,
Where in a score years will you be,
  And the delicate succubae you kissed?

Idols and images, every one,
  Crash down like ancient theory;
Where is the Vortex under the sun
  That spins not always emptily?
Cease these jeers at minstrelsy,
  You, who perish and are not missed,
For where in a score years will you be,
  And the delicate succubae you kissed?

L'Envoi

Pound, though your henchmen now agree
To hail the Prince in the Anarchist,
Where in a score years will you be,
And the pale pink dream blown mouths you
kissed?

FROM THE CHAPBOOK:
A MONTHLY MISCELLANY
MAY 1921

Pathology des Dommagistes

(Being specimens for a projected Anthology to be issued in the
USA)

'C'est vrai, c'est dommage,
et c'est dommage c'est vrai.'

(Translated from the Elizabethan by B.H.W.)

Epigram
(after the Cretan)

Little Caligulala
Has tied one golden sandal
Round her pink ankle
Too tightly.
Heu! The discomfort
The varicose veins ...

Silver dust falls
Over the tepidarium ...

Selected Bulbs from a Javan Pot

Wondering when I would be able to pay my
laundress, I let my eyes fall and I saw the
smutty tamarinds I grow in my little window-box.

'Conticuerunt Omnes'

Lesbia's hair
Swathing her navel
Has been dyed with henna
To match the goldfish
In the plashing fountain?

'Tutti Frutti'

On the spots of
The brown cushion
My love
Has laid her yellow hairs.

Her fan is not moving:

Where
Is the drunken juggler?

NOTES

Abbreviated titles of the main sources of reference;

T.L.S.: *The Times Literary Supplement* (London).

Poetry: *Poetry* (Chicago).

T.E.H.: *T. E. Hulme* by Michael Roberts: Faber & Faber, 1938.

T.N.A.: *The New Age* (London).

EG: The *Egoist* (London).

Paige: *The Letters of Ezra Pound: 1907–1941*, Ed. D. D. Paige, New York, Harcourt, Brace & Co., 1950.

Aldington: *Life for Life's Sake*, by Richard Aldington, Cassell & Co., 1968.

T.L.R.: *The Little Review* (Chicago).

F.N.R.: *The Fortnightly Review* (London).

SPEC: *Speculations* by T. E. Hulme, Ed. Herbert Read, Routledge & Kegan Paul, 1960.

W.C.W.: *Autobiography* by William Carlos Williams, New York, New Directions Paperback, 1967.

N.A.P.: *The New American Poetry*, Ed. Donald M. Allen, Evergreen Books; New York, Grove Press, 1960.

1. See *Georgian Poetry*, Ed. James Reeves: Penguin, 1962.
2. Delivered at Washington University, St Louis, Missouri, 9 June 1953. Printed in *To Criticize the Critic*, Faber & Faber, 1965.
3. T.L.S. 11 January 1917.
4. 'On Impressionism', *Poetry*, August 1913.
5. Quoted in *Ezra Pound: A Close-Up* by Michael Reck, Rupert Hart-Davies, 1968, pp. 14–15.
6. In the first edition of Ezra Pound, *Personae*, Elkin Matthews, 1909.
7. T.E.H. p. 266.
8. T.N.A. IV 11 February 1909, p. 327.
9. 'History of Imagism', EG 1 May 1915.

10. T.E.H. p. 269.
11. Paige, p. 6.
12. See *Ezra Pound's Kensington* by Patricia Hutchins: Faber & Faber, 1965, p. 36.
13. *Imagist Anthology 1930*, 'Those Were the Days', Chatto & Windus, 1930, p.xiii.
14. Aldington, p. 123.
15. Paige, p. 11. London, October 1912.
16. *Criterion* II, 7 April 1924, pp. 231–2.
17. Paige, p. 213. Rapallo, 26 September 1927.
18. T.L.R. July 1914, 'Des Imagistes', p. 15.
19. The *Review* (London), April 1965, 'Documents on Imagism from the Papers of F. S. Flint', Ed. Christopher Middleton.
20. 3 July 1915.
21. Paige, p. 48. Coleman's Hatch, January 1915.
22. F.N.R. September 1914, p. 468.
23. ibid. p. 461–2.
24. ibid. p. 463–4.
25. Aldington, p. 127.
26. *The Literature of the United States* by Marcus Cunliffe: Penguin, 1966, p. 268.
27. Aldington, p. 127.
28. Paige, p. 38. London, 1 August 1914.
29. Aldington, p. 123–4.
30. Paige, p. 39. London, 12 August 1914.
31. ibid. p. 44. London, 19 October 1914.
32. Paige, pp.113–44. London, August 1917 (to Margaret C. Anderson – ed. of T.L.R.).
33. *Contemporary Literature*, Autumn 1969, University of Wisconsin Press.
34. New York, Macmillan, 1917, p. 255.
35. 'Miss Lowell's Discovery', *Poetry*, April 1915, p. 35.
36. Preface to *Preludes and Symphonies*, New York, Macmillan,1930.
37. Paige, p. 212. Rapallo, 26 September 1927.
38. From 'Wedding Morn': I am indebted to Glenn Hughes for this story in his *Imagism and the Imagists*, O.U.P., 1931, p. 169.

39. Aldington, p. 127.

40. Paige, p. 212. Rapallo, 26 September 1927.

41. Preface to the American edition of *New Poems by D. H. Lawrence* – reprinted in *Phoenix*, Heinemann, 1956.

42. Hueffer in *Outlook*, 10 July 1915.

43. 'Tradition and the Individual Talent' (1919) from *Selected Essays*: Faber & Faber, 1961, p. 17.

44. Aldington, pp. 130–31.

45. op. cit. p. xviii.

46. Pt. II: Chapter 5. (Printed in *Stony Brook*, New York, 1969).

47. *The Philosophy of Schopenhauer*, New York, Random House, 1956, p. 146: quoted by L. S. Dembo in his *Conceptions of Reality in Modern American Poetry*, University of California Press, 1966, p. 2.

48. *Le Bovarysme*, Jules de Gaultier, Paris, 1892.

49. *Matière et Mémoire*, Henri Bergson, Paris, 1896.

50. *Essai sur l'Imagination Créatrice*, Théodule Ribot, Paris, 1900 (trans. by Baron, Kegan Paul, 1906).

51. *Le Problème du Style*, Rémy de Gourmont, Paris, 1902.

52. See *Ezra Pound's Poetics and Literary Tradition* by N. Christoph de Nagy, Bern, 1966 pp. 70–72.

53. SPEC p. 116.

54. SPEC p. 127.

55. SPEC p. 126.

56. SPEC p. 122.

57. SPEC p. 133.

58. SPEC p. 120.

59. SPEC p. 144.

60. *An Introduction to Metaphysics* by Henri Bergson (trans. by T. E. Hulme, London, 1913) p. 14.

61. T.E.H. p. 269.

62. T.E.H. p. 268.

63. SPEC p. 229.

64. T.E.H. p. 285.

65. *Selected Essays*, op. cit. p. 22.

66. 'The Imagists Discussed': EG 1 May 1915.

67. 'The Place of Imagism', *New Republic*, 22 May 1915.
68. Letter to J. C. Squire, 29 January 1917.
69. 'The Later Yeats': *Poetry*, May 1914: reprinted in *Literary Essays of Ezra Pound*, Ed. T. S. Eliot, Faber & Faber, 1960, p. 380.
70. EG 1 June 1915.
71. T.E.H. p. 281.
72. T.E.H. p. 297.
73. F.N.R. September 1914, p. 466.
74. EG 1 May 1915.
75. F.N.R. September 1914, p. 467: and *Gaudier-Brzeska*, London, 1916, p. 103.
76. *Life is My Song*, Farrar & Rinehart, 1937, pp. 213–14.
77. Eunice Tietjens in T.L.R. November 1914.
78. Margaret C. Anderson in T.L.R. August 1915.
79. John Gould Fletcher in T.L.R. April 1915.
80. Huntley Carter in T.L.R. September 1915.
81. Lewis Worthington Smith in *Atlantic Monthly*, April 1916.
82. *The Chapbook: A Monthly Miscellany*, May 1921.
83. *Nation*, 24 February 1916.
84. 18 September–9 October (4 parts) 1915: 'The New Poetry – A Critique'.
85. The *New Statesman*, 3 March 1917.
86. The *New Statesman*, 24 March 1917.
87. *Nation*, 24 February 1916.
88. Amy Lowell interviewed in *New York Times*, 26 March 1916.
89. *Poetry*, March 1918, by Alice Corbin Henderson.
90. Harold Monro, 'The Imagists Discussed', EG 1 May 1915.
91. SPEC p. 131.
92. 'The New Poetry – A Critique', op. cit.
93. *Outlook*, 10 July 1915.
94. *Poetry*, December 1914: in a review of Emily Dickinson's *The Single Hound*.
95. W.C.W: p. 264.
96. Printed in *Stony Brook*, 1/2 Fall, New York, 1968.
97. Preface to *Some Imagist Poets 1915*.

98. W.C.W. p. 264.

99. Preface to *Some Imagist Poets 1916*.

100. From 'A Young American Poet' in T.L.R. March 1915. (Flint also used the phrase of H.D.'s poetry in E G 1 May 1915.)

101. N.A.P. p. 413.

102. Wallace Stevens: *Opus Posthumous:* Faber & Faber, 1959, p. 164.

103. W.C.W. p. 390.

104. T.E.H. p. 269–70.

105. From *A Marianne Moore Reader:* reprinted in *Modern Poets on Modern Poetry*, Ed. James Scully, Fontana, 1966, p. 107.

106. On 'Hamlet' (1919) in *Selected Essays*, op. cit. p. 145.

107. SPEC p. 144.

108. Mifflin (1916) and Constable (1918).

109. Allen Wingate, 1948, p. 16.

110. See Wallace Martin's article on 'Freud and Imagism' in *Notes and Queries*, December 1916, p. 471.

111. T.N.A. XVI, 28 January 1915, p. 349.

112. F.N.R. September 1914, p. 103.

113. *Poetry*, January 1958, p. 256 in a review of *Selected Poems of H.D.*

114. Section IV.

115. Faber & Faber, 1959, pp. 9–10.

116. N.A.P. pp. 387–8.

117. *Palimpsest*, pt II. (*Murex*), Southern Illinois University Press, 1968, p. 154.

118. *Bid Me To Live*, New York, Grove Press, 1963, p. 89.

119. *Selected Essays*, New York, Random House, 1954, p. 122.

120. Introduction to *Collected Poems* printed in *Modern Poets on Modern Poetry*, op. cit., p. 124.

121. From a review of *Imagist Anthology 1930* in T.L.S. 25 June 1931.

BIOGRAPHICAL NOTES

Richard (*Edward Godfree*) *Aldington*
(pp. 53-8; 107-8)

Was born in Portsmouth, Hampshire, on 8 July 1892, the son of a solicitor. He studied for four years at Dover College and for one year at the University of London. By the age of 19 he read Greek, Latin, French and Italian with ease. The added good fortune of having access to his father's library which contained many volumes of poetry prepared him at the age of 18 to launch a creative attack on poetic tradition. His own first volume of poems appeared when he was 17. In 1913 he married H.D. and became a founder member of the imagist movement. Together, he and H.D. translated from Greek and Latin, bringing out a volume entitled *Images, Old and New* (1915). He edited the periodical *Egoist*, contributing essays on French poetry and philosophy. He joined Ezra Pound and Wyndham Lewis in their efforts to shake the complacent literary world through the magazine *Blast*. In 1916 he enlisted in the Infantry, returning shell-shocked and unsettled from the war. He lived thereafter mainly in France and Italy, earning a living from reviewing and writing articles on French literature for *The Times Literary Supplement*. His marriage to H.D. was dissolved in 1937.

At the time of his death in 1962 he was best known for his 1914-18 war novel, *Death of a Hero*. It was then a best-seller in Russia. Other than his imagist poetry, his best-known poem is 'A Dream in the Luxembourg' – an evocation of the 1920s. His *Life of Wellington* won the James Tait Black Memorial Prize in 1946. It was followed by his study of D. H. Lawrence, *Portrait of a Genius . . . but* in 1950 and *Lawrence of Arabia* in 1953, both books expressing the sense of rebellion still alive in him. His autobiography, *Life for Life's Sake*, was published in 1968.

Harriet Monroe said he looked like a footballer and Amy Lowell described him as a dyed-in-the-wool Britisher, but he would have preferred *The Times* obituary notice: 'An angry young man of the generation before they became fashionable, he remained something of an angry old man to the end.'

Skipwith Cannell
(pp. 59 (47, 60, 98))

Is most elusive. When Aldington came to compile the *Imagist Anthology 1930* he wrote: '[The anthology] contained poems by everyone who had contributed [to the earlier anthologies] (including James Joyce and William Carlos Williams) except poor Amy who was dead, Skipwith Cannell whom we couldn't trace, and Ezra who was sulky.' Cannell remains elusive, as do Edward Storer, Allen Upward and John Cournos, about whom there seems to be little biographical data of relevance to the Imagists.

H.D. (Hilda Doolittle)
(pp. 61-9; 109-13)

Was born in Bethlehem, Pennsylvania (USA) in 1886, the daughter of the director of the Flower Astronomical Observatory at the University of Pennsylvania. She saw a good deal of Ezra Pound and William Carlos Williams during the period of her education at Bryn Mawr. She was first in print as the writer of stories for children in a Presbyterian paper in 1906 – an experience that looked ahead to the publication of her children's book *The Hedgehog* (1936). Her visit to Europe for the summer of 1911 became life-long. In 1912, at the time of the founding of the imagist movement, she met Richard Aldington and married him in the following year. A series of tragedies confirmed her withdrawal into the past. In 1915 Aldington went to fight in France and she took over his strenuous duties as assistant editor of the *Egoist*. In the same year she had a miscarriage of her first child. In 1918 her favourite brother was killed in France and a year later her father died. She separated from Aldington although they were not divorced until 1937. In 1920 the birth of her second child, a daughter, was accompanied by double pneumonia, and she suffered a breakdown. She was psychoanalysed by Freud (1933-4) and recounted her experiences in her *Tribute to Freud* (1944). In 1938 she had won the Helen Haire Levinson Prize for poetry, but it was during the Second World War, which she spent in London, that her poetry reached its full flowering in the writing of her war trilogy, *The Walls Do Not Fall* (1944), *Tribute To The Angels* (1945), and *The Flowering Of The Rod* (1946). She was the first woman to receive the Award of Merit Medal for Poetry from the American Academy of Arts and Letters (1960). Although mostly known for her short Hellenistic poems, she was a novelist of considerable stature and it is in her novels that her personality appears – they are in the main autobiographical. She completed her final book, a poem of length entitled *Helen in Egypt*, in Switzerland in 1960. She died there in 1961.

John Gould Fletcher
(pp. 70–74, 114–16)

Was born in 1886 in Little Rock, Arkansas (USA). He studied at Harvard but left without taking a degree. Like Aldington's, his individualism was too strong – he could not stand academic training. He learned French, however, and developed a passion for French poetry. He settled to write in Boston, but became restless, and after inheriting an income sufficient to allow him to devote his life to literature, he moved to Europe and lived there from 1908 to 1933, when he returned to his native Arkansas. He died there in 1950.

In London he existed as a recluse. Unable to find a publisher, he paid for publication of five small volumes of his poetry in 1913. Ezra Pound encouraged him with a perceptive review in the *New Freewoman*, commending the French influence, the individuality of rhythm, the poet's courage in going 'to the dustbin for his subjects'. His book of poems *Irradiations* (1915) shows his imagist leanings, and his *Goblins and Pagodas* (1916) contains experimental efforts particularly in polyphonic prose. His other poetic experiments include the 'Symphonies' – written in 1914–15. Among his prose works the best known are his *Paul Gauguin* (1921) and his autobiography, *Life Is My Song* (1937). His *Selected Poems* won him the Pulitzer Prize for 1939.

Frank Stuart Flint
(pp. 75-80, 129-30, 143-9)

Was born in Islington in 1885, the son of a commercial traveller. His boyhood was spent in squalid poverty and even before he left elementary school he spent evenings working as a barber's lather-boy. He left school at 13 and took any odd job that came his way. Eventually he joined the Civil Service as a typist at 19, studying Latin and French at night school. Later he mastered, without instruction, ten languages. He gradually gained a reputation as the authority on modern French poetry in London. In 1909 he married and privately published his first poems – love lyrics dedicated to his wife – *In The Net Of The Stars*. They were romantic, derivative poems, but tending towards new freedom of form. After his meeting with T. E. Hulme and Ezra Pound, his poetry changed and became more imagistic in the volume *Cadences* (1915), composed mainly in free verse, or what he called 'unrimed cadence'. But it is noteworthy that his third volume, *Otherworld: Cadences*, reverted to his natural vein of romanticism.

He served in the army in 1918–19, and later became Chief of Overseas Section, Statistics Division, while still maintaining a steady flow of articles, translations and reviews in the *Chapbook*, the *Egoist*, *Poetry Review* and *The Times Literary Supplement*. He was one of the most dedicated and sincere of the Imagists. Sadly there was no revival of his poetic impulse after *Otherworlds* and for this reason, perhaps, he is omitted, shamefully, from the *Oxford Companion to English Literature*, although his writings on French poetry alone should earn him a place. When he retired from the Ministry of Labour in 1951, he was awarded the Imperial Service Order. He died on 29 February 1960.

Ford Madox Ford
(pp. 81-2)

Was born in 1873, son of Dr Francis Hueffer, music critic of *The Times* in the 1880s. His mother was the daughter of Ford Madox Brown, the artist. Among his early works were a volume of poems (published when he was 20 years old), a life of Ford Madox Brown, and several historical novels. He founded the *English Review* in 1908, to which Thomas Hardy, Henry James, H. G. Wells, and John Galsworthy, among others, contributed. He was also closely associated with Joseph Conrad and collaborated with him in the writing of *Romance* and *The Inheritors*. His biography of Conrad is a notable work, and among his best novels are *Vive le Roy* and *The Marsden Case*. He also wrote a fine critical study of Henry James and one of Rossetti. He served in France in the First World War. He died at Deauville, France, on 26 June 1939.

Thomas Ernest Hulme
(pp. 48–9)

Was born in 1883 at Gratton Hall, his family home, in the village of Endon, Staffordshire. In 1901 he was elected to an exhibition at St John's College, Cambridge, to read mathematics. He was sent down in 1904 after undefined disturbances and was given the 'longest mock funeral ever seen in the town'. Always impatient of authority (a trait common to the Imagists), after a trial run at University College, London, to study Biology and Physics, he continued to journey to Cambridge to attend philosophy lectures. In 1906 he gave up and went to Canada where he began to sense the 'chasm' between man and God, '... the fright of the mind before the unknown'. He returned to Europe, going to Brussels to study the philosophers Bergson, Gourmont and de Gaultier. In 1908 he formed the Poets' Club in London and later, with Pound and Flint as members, a club that met at the Eiffel Tower restaurant in Soho. It was here that he talked of and read his own poems, explaining his theory of 'the image' in poetry. He published a series of articles on Bergson in 1911 in *New Age*, where the so-called 'Complete Poetical Works of T. E. Hulme' were published as well, in January 1912. Pound reprinted them as an appendix to his *Ripostes* in April 1912.

The comprehensive complete poems are printed in A. R. Jones's *The Life and Opinions of T. E. Hulme* (1960). Hulme also published translations of works by Sorel and Bergson, and wrote the influential prose works *Speculations* and *Notes on Language and Style*. He planned extensive further work as well, but was killed in action in 1917.

James (*Augustine Aloysius*) Joyce
(pp. 83)

Was born at Rathgar, Dublin, on 2 February 1882, and died in Zurich on 13 January 1941. One of a large poor family, he went to the National University of Ireland in Dublin to study Modern Languages and graduated in 1902. He developed a passion for Ibsen's works and learned Norwegian to read him in the original. Dissatisfied with the bigotry of Catholicism as he saw it, he left Ireland to spend the rest of his life chiefly in Paris, Trieste, and Zurich. His first published work was *Chamber Music* (1907), from which 'I hear an army' – included by Pound in his *Des Imagistes* – was taken. In 1914 came *Dubliners*, a book of stories delayed nine years by the publishers who wanted to omit certain offending passages. His *Portrait of the Artist as a Young Man* was serialized by Pound in the *Egoist*, 1914–15. At that time Joyce had already begun to write *Ulysses* in Trieste. This was serialized in *The Little Review* from March 1915 to August 1920, when it was suppressed by a prosecution instigated by the Society for the Suppression of Vice. The complete novel was published in Paris and by the Egoist Press in London in 1922.

David Herbert Lawrence
(pp. 84-6, 117-19)

Was born on 11 September 1885, at Eastwood in Nottinghamshire, the son of a coal miner. He spent 'three years savage teaching of collier lads' and then went by scholarship to Nottingham University and on to teach in Croydon. He abandoned teaching for writing after the publication of his first novel, *The White Peacock*, in 1911. It was this novel Ford Madox Ford encouraged, along with some of Lawrence's poems sent to him surreptitiously by a friend of Lawrence, when he was editor of the *English Review*. His association with the Imagists was brief – he never became a convinced Imagist. Primarily known as a novelist and short-story writer, his collections of poems are numerous and include *Love Poems and Others* (1913), *Amores* (1916), *New Poems* (1918), and *Bay* (1919). *Birds, Beasts and Flowers* was begun in Tuscany in 1920 and finished in New Mexico in 1923. Of his volume *Pansies* (1929), he wrote in words reminiscent of Imagist practice, '... they are rather *Pensées* than anything else. Pascal or La Bruyère wrote their *Pensées* in prose, but it has always seemed to me that a real thought, a single thought, not an argument, can only exist in verse, or in some poetic form.' *Nettles* appeared in 1930 and his *Last Poems* (1930) were edited posthumously by Richard Aldington. In his introduction to that volume Aldington wrote: 'Lawrence's writing was not something outside himself, it was part of himself, it came out of his life and in turn fed his life.'

Amy Lowell
(pp. 87-90, 120-21)

Was born in Brookline, Massachusetts (USA) in 1874, a collateral descendant of James Russell Lowell. Educated privately, she travelled widely even as a child. Her first book of poems, *A Dome of Many-coloured Glass* (1912), was trite and conventional; but after meeting and later managing the Imagists in London (1915) her work took on a zest and a search for experimental forms which never left her. Her two-volume biography of Keats occupied her later years, though she still found time to write poems, lecture, and give readings. Her experimentation led her to polyphonic prose, which became one of the by-ways of Imagism. Her passions for Keats, Japanese art and colourful gardens show throughout her writing.

She was so energetic and prolific that her book, *Men, Women and Ghosts* (1916), contains 360 pages of verse, yet she says in her Preface that she has excluded all purely lyrical forms written in that period. From her later years, besides the Keats biography, she left manuscripts sufficient for three volumes of poetry. They were published posthumously as *What's O'Clock* (awarded the Pulitzer Prize for 1925), *East Wind* and *Ballads for Sale*. She is celebrated for her eccentricities, among others smoking cigars and sleeping on sixteen pillows. In spite of D. H. Lawrence's stricture that 'in everything she did she was a good amateur', there is a sense of vitality, dedication, and conscientious craftsmanship about most of her work. She died in 1925.

Marianne Craig Moore
(pp. 91-2)

Was born in St Louis, Missouri (USA) in 1887. After her education at Bryn Mawr, she taught shorthand, before becoming an assistant in the New York Public Library (1921-5). She has lived mainly in New York, and it was from there that she edited *The Dial* (1925-9). Her association with the Imagists was through the columns of the *Egoist* where some of her early poems appeared, but she was never a card-carrying Imagist. She won the Dial award for her second book of poetry and her *Collected Poems* (1951) was awarded the Pulitzer Prize. She also translated *The Fables of La Fontaine* (1954). She died in 1972.

Ezra Loomis Pound
(pp. 93-7, 130-34, 141-2)

Was born in Idaho (USA) in 1885 and came to Europe in 1908. In Italy he published his first volume of poems, *A Lume Spento* (1908). He settled then in London until 1920 – during that time publishing *Personae* (1909), *Canzoni* (1911), *Ripostes* (1912), *Cathay* (Chinese translations) (1916), and *Hugh Selwyn Mauberley* (1920). While in London he helped found the imagist movement and then went over to the Vorticists and became involved with Wyndham Lewis in the magazine *Blast*. In 1920 he left England for Paris and Italy, and settled in Rapallo in 1924, where he began his long poem, the *Cantos*, which has occupied him until the present day. He was discredited for his Fascist broadcasts during the Second World War and tried for treason in the United States in 1946. Acquitted as of unsound mind, he was confined in Washington to a mental hospital. He was released in 1961 and returned to Italy. He was given the Dial award in 1928 for his contribution to American letters and he was awarded the Bollingen Prize in 1949.

William Carlos Williams
(pp. 99–103; 122–5)

Was born in Rutherford, New Jersey (USA) in 1883. He studied
medicine in Geneva, Pennsylvania and at Leipzig. In 1910 he settled
in Rutherford where he practised as a doctor. His *Poems* (1909) and
The Tempers (1913) employ the techniques of Imagism, but he soon
began to launch his own campaign to 'create somehow by an intense,
individual effort, a new – an American – poetic language'. In 1920
he wrote, 'I'll write whatever I damn please, whenever I damn please,
and as I damn please . . .' Like the other original Imagists he became a
strong individualist. In 1926 he was given the Dial award for dis-
tinguished service to American literature, and his *Pictures from
Bruegel and Other Poems* was awarded the Pulitzer Prize. Always
attracted by the idea of an *American* epic, he wrote *Paterson* in four
volumes between 1946 and 1951, the year of his *Autobiography*. He
also wrote many short stories and novels, but in prose he was at his
best as a critic, particularly in his book *In the American Grain* (1925).
He died in 1963.

SELECTED BIBLIOGRAPHY OF
WORKS MENTIONED
(Place of publication London unless otherwise stated)

Des Imagistes, Poetry Bookshop, 1914; New York, Albert and Charles
Boni, 1914.
Some Imagist Poets (3 vols), Constable, 1915, 1916, 1917; Boston,
Houghton Mifflin, 1915, 1916, 1917.
Imagist Anthology 1930, Chatto & Windus, 1930.

ALDINGTON, RICHARD: *Images, 1910–1915*, Poetry Bookshop,
1915. *Images*, Egoist Press, 1919. *Images of War*, Allen & Unwin,
1919. *Complete Poems*, Allen Wingate, 1948. *Life for Life's Sake*,
Cassell, 1968.
CUMMINGS, E. E.: *Complete Poems* (2 vols) MacGibbon & Kee, 1968.

FLETCHER, JOHN GOULD: *Irradiations: Sand and Spray*, Boston, Houghton Mifflin, 1915; Constable, 1915. *Preludes and Symphonies*, New York, Macmillan, 1930. *Life Is My Song*, New York, Farrar & Rinehart, 1937.

FLINT, F. S.: *In The Net Of The Stars*, Elkin Matthews, 1909. *Cadences*, Poetry Bookshop, 1915. *Otherworld: Cadences*, Poetry Bookshop, 1920.

H.D. (HILDA DOOLITTLE): *Collected Poems*, New York, Boni & Liveright, 1925 and 1940. *Selected Poems*, New York, Grove Press, 1957. *Red Roses For Bronze*, Chatto & Windus, 1931. *The Walls Do Not Fall*, O.U.P., 1944. *Tribute To The Angels*, O.U.P., 1945. *The Flowering Of The Rod*, O.U.P., 1946. *Helen in Egypt*, New York, Grove Press, 1961. *Palimpsest*, Southern Illinois, 1968. *Bid Me To Live*, New York, Grove Press, 1963. *Tribute to Freud*, Oxford, Carcanet Press, 1971. *Ion of Euripides*, Chatto & Windus, 1937.

HULME, T. E.: *Speculations*, Ed. Herbert Read: Routledge & Kegan Paul, 1960. 'Lecture on Modern Poetry', in Michael Roberts's *T. E. Hulme*, Carcanet, 1982. Poems included in *The Life and Opinions of T. E. Hulme* by Alun R. Jones, Gollancz, 1960.

LAWRENCE, D. H.: *The Complete Poems* (2 vols), Heinemann, 1967.

LOWELL, AMY: *The Complete Poetical Works*, Boston, Houghton Mifflin, 1955.

MOORE, MARIANNE: *Collected Poems*, Faber & Faber, 1951.

POUND, EZRA: *Ripostes*, Stephen Swift & Co. Ltd., 1912. *Selected Poems* (intro. by T. S. Eliot), Faber & Faber, London, 1948. *Collected Shorter Poems*, Faber & Faber, 1952. *Cantos*, Faber & Faber, 1968. *Literary Essays* (edited and introduced by T. S. Eliot), Faber & Faber, 1954. *Letters (1907–1941)*, Ed. D. D. Paige: New York, Harcourt, Brace & Co., 1950; Faber & Faber, 1951.

STORER, EDWARD: *Mirrors of Illusion*, 1909.

WILLIAMS, WILLIAM CARLOS: *Collected Earlier Poems:* MacGibbon & Kee, 1951; New York, New Directions, 1951. *Paterson*, Bks I–V: MacGibbon & Kee, 1964; New York, New Directions, 1963. *Autobiography*, New York, New Directions, 1967; MacGibbon & Kee, 1968.

FURTHER READING

ALLEN, Donald M. (Ed.), *The New American Poetry*, New York, Grove Press, 1960.

COFFMAN, Stanley K., *Imagism: A Chapter for the History of Modern Poetry*, Oklahoma, Norman, 1951.

CUNLIFFE, Marcus, *The Literature of the United States*, Penguin, 1954.

DEMBO, L. S., *Conceptions of Reality in Modern American Poetry*, California, Berkeley, 1966.

GRANT, Joy, *Harold Monro and The Poetry Bookshop*, Routledge & Kegan Paul, 1967.

H.D., *End to Torment: A Memoir of Ezra Pound*, Carcanet, 1980.

HOUGH, Graham, *Image and Experience*, Duckworth, 1960.

HUGHES, Glenn, *Imagism and the Imagists: A Study in Modern Poetry*, California, Stanford U.P., 1931.

HUTCHINS, Patricia, *Ezra Pound's Kensington*, Faber & Faber, 1965.

JONES, Alun R., *The Life and Opinions of T. E. Hulme*, Gollancz, 1960. *Imagism: A Unity of Gesture*, in *American Poetry*: Stratford-on-Avon Studies, No. 7, Arnold, 1965.

JONES, Peter, *An Introduction to Fifty American Poets*, Pan Books, 1979.

READ, Herbert, *The True Voice of Feeling*, Faber & Faber, 1968.

RECK, Michael, *Ezra Pound: A Close-Up*, Rupert Hart-Davis, 1968.

REEVES, James (Ed.), *Georgian Poetry*, Penguin, 1962.

ROBERTS, Michael, *T. E. Hulme*, Carcanet, 1982.

ROSS, Robert H., *The Georgian Revolt*, Faber & Faber, 1967.

SCHMIDT, Michael, *An Introduction to Fifty British Poets, 1300–1900*, Pan Books, 1979. *An Introduction to Fifty Modern British Poets*, Pan Books, 1979.

SCULLEY, James (Ed.), *Modern Poets on Modern Poetry*, Fontana, 1966.

SISSON, C. H., *English Poetry 1900–1950, an Assessment*, Carcanet, 1981.

STEAD, C. K., *The New Poetic: Yeats to Eliot*, Penguin, 1964.

STOCK, Noel, *The Life of Ezra Pound*, Routledge & Kegan Paul, 1970.

YOUNG, Alan, *Dada and After*, Manchester University Press, 1981.

ACKNOWLEDGEMENTS

For permission to reprint the works in this anthology acknowledge-
ment is made to the following: for Conrad Aiken: 'Ballade of
Worshippers of the Image' from the New York *Sun*, 9 May 1915, to
the author. For Richard Aldington: 'Au Vieux Jardin', 'Epigrams',
'Amalfi', 'Images', 'Sunsets', 'To a Greek Marble', 'Picket',
'Insouciance', 'Living Sepulchres', 'Evening', and sections I and VII
from 'Passages Toward a Long Poem', from *Complete Poems*, Allen
Wingate, 1948; and brief extracts from *Life for Life's Sake*, Cassell,
1968, to Mme Catherine Guillaume. Copyright © Catherine
Guillaume, 1972. For H.D. (Hilda Doolittle): Sections I, II, III, IV
from *The Flowering of the Rod*, O.U.P., 1946, to Norman Holmes
Pearson; 'If You Will Let Me Sing' from *Imagist Anthology 1930*,
Chatto & Windus, 1930, and 'Epitaph' from *Red Roses For Bronze*,
Chatto & Windus, 1931, to Norman Holmes Pearson; 'Oread',
'Evening', 'Sitalkas', 'Hermes of the Ways', 'The Garden', 'The
Pool', 'Sea Rose', parts 3 and 4 of 'Iphegeneia' from *Collected
Poems of HD*, Liveright Publishing Corporation, 1925, to Norman
Holmes Pearson. Copyright © 1925, 1953 by Norman Holmes
Pearson. For John Gould Fletcher: 'Demolition of the Waldorf-
Astoria' from *Imagist Anthology 1930*, Chatto & Windus, 1930, to
the author's Literary Estate and Chatto & Windus, Ltd. For F. S.
Flint: 'London', 'Beggar', 'November', 'Cones', 'Searchlight',
'Soldiers', 'The Swan', from *Cadences*, Poetry Bookshop, 1915; 'A
Swan Song' from *In The Net Of The Stars*, Elkin Matthews, 1909; 'To
a Young Lady who Moved Shyly Among Men' from *Otherworld:
Cadences*, Poetry Bookshop, 1920; 'Imagisme' from *Poetry*, March
1913 and Letter to J. C. Squire printed in *Review* No. 15, 1965, to
Mrs Ianthe Price. For Ford Madox Ford: extract from 'Antwerp' Part
IV, from *The Bodley Head Ford Madox Ford* Volume I, to The
Bodley Head, London. For T. E. Hulme: 'Autumn', 'Above the
Dock', 'Conversion', 'The Sunset', 'The Man in the Crow's Nest',

and 'Images' from *The Life and Opinions of T. E. Hulme* by A. R. Jones, 1960, to Victor Gollancz Ltd. For James Joyce: 'I Hear an Army' from *Chamber Music* Jonathan Cape Ltd, to the Executors of the James Joyce Estate. For D. H. Lawrence: 'Autumn Rain', 'Ultimate Reality', 'Nothing to Save', 'Listen to the Band!', 'Green', 'At the Window', 'Brooding Grief', 'Intimates', 'Image-Making Love', and 'Illicit' (later titled 'On The Balcony') from *The Complete Poems of D. H. Lawrence*, William Heinemann Ltd, to Laurence Pollinger Ltd, and to the estate of the late Mrs Frieda Lawrence. For Amy Lowell: 'In a Garden', 'Spring Day' (extract,) 'Streets', 'Yoshiwara Lament', 'Circumstance', 'Autumn', 'Illusion', 'Autumn Haze', 'Middle Age', 'Wind and Silver', 'Fugitive', 'If I Were Francesco Guardi', from *The Complete Poetical Works of Amy Lowell*, Houghton Mifflin Co., Boston, to Houghton Mifflin Co. For Marianne Moore: 'A Talisman', 'He Made This Screen', and 'You Are Like the Realistic Product of an Idealistic Search for Gold at the Foot of the Rainbow' (later retitled 'To a Chameleon') to the author. For Ezra Pound: 'The Return', 'After Ch'u Yuan', 'Liu Ch'e', 'Fan-piece, for Her Imperial Lord', 'Ts'ai Chi'h' 'In A Station Of The Metro', 'The Garden', 'Alba', 'Heather', 'Albatre', 'The Encounter', 'A Girl' from *Collected Shorter Poems*, Faber & Faber; and Letter to Harriet Monroe, from *Letters of Ezra Pound*, Faber & Faber; and the extract from 'A Few Don'ts by an Imagiste', from *Literary Essays of Ezra Pound*, Faber & Faber, to Faber & Faber Ltd. For Charles Reznikoff: 'From My Window' from *By the Waters of Manhattan*, Fulcrum Press, to the author. For William Carlos Williams: 'Postlude', 'Fire Spirit', 'To Mark Anthony In Heaven', 'Portrait of a Lady', 'The Shadow', 'Metric Figure', 'Summer Song', 'Autumn', 'Rain', from *The Collected Earlier Poems*, MacGibbon & Kee, to New Directions Publishing Corporation. For Prefaces to *Some Imagist Poets 1915 & 1916* (unsigned) to Constable & Co. Ltd.

INDEX OF AUTHORS,
TITLES AND FIRST LINES